Acquiring Competencies
to Teach Mathematics
in Elementary Schools

by

L. Y. Hollis

Love Yvorne

Professor of Curriculum and Instruction
University of Houston

and

W. Robert Houston

Professor of Curriculum and Instruction
University of Houston

PROFESSIONAL EDUCATORS PUBLICATIONS, INC.
LINCOLN, NEBRASKA

Library of Congress Catalog Card No.: 72-89057

ISBN   0-88224-032-3

© Copyright 1973
by
Professional Educators Publications, Inc.

Acquiring Competencies to Teach
Mathematics in Elementary Schools

THE PROFESSIONAL EDUCATION SERIES

Walter K. Beggs, *Editor*
Dean Emeritus Teachers College, and
Professor of Educational Administration
University of Nebraska

Royce H. Knapp, *Research Editor*
Regents Professor of Education
Teachers College
University of Nebraska

Contents

Preface

The flight of the Russian satellite Sputnik, in 1957, stimulated American education to greater emphasis on mathematics and the sciences. Within two years the mathematics profession had initiated several projects to design new curricula for American children. They were more vigorous, more precise, more coordinated from kindergarten through college. New language and content was introduced, for example, set theory, non-metric geometry, properties, arrays, and binary numerals. These concepts for the most part were alien to both parents and teachers; while hailed by mathematicians as a giant step forward, the average person applauded what he could not understand.

In the intervening years, the first wave of children to complete their education in the post-Sputnik era have graduated from high school. Massive doses of in-service education, new text materials, and creative ideas have been introduced into the elementary school program. The "New Math" is no longer so strange, and recent developments have increased the scope and power of mathematics instruction.

The mathematics laboratory blossomed in England and is being adopted by many in this country. Rather than studying algorithms in a textbook, children explore and solve problems, and in doing so learn the salient aspects of mathematics.

Instructional materials are commonplace. Many elementary children employ Cuisenaire rods, Stern blocks, abaci, attribute blocks, and other aides in learning mathematics. The range of creative effort and the extent to which the teacher can deviate from traditional patterns for teaching mathematics has so increased to make this a uniquely challenging subject to teach.

A related movement in teacher education is significantly altering preparation programs and certification requirements. Competency-based teacher education requires the instructor to specify his objectives in advance, list them in terms of what the learner will be able to do upon completion, and tailor instruction to those objectives. Further, objectives should be relevant to the tasks a teacher performs.

This volume combines and articulates the confluence of these two movements. The competencies of elementary teachers which seem most relevant to being effective teachers of mathematics have been identified and specified. Then the tenets of effective instruction and the most recent concepts of mathematics education are succinctly outlined for the reader. This brevity yet comprehensiveness of major aspects of instruction will make this a useful introduction and continuing guide to facilitating the mathematical development of children.

Assessment of Competency in the Mathematics Taught in the Elementary School

There is a saying, "You cannot teach something you do not know, any more than you can come back from some place you have never been." It is important for the elementary school teacher of mathematics to know and understand that which is being taught. This competency should be at a level that will enable the teacher to provide an enriched program that is specified in textbook materials. This requires an understanding of the basic principles of mathematics, which is necessary if the teacher is to individualize program goals and objectives.

The following test is designed to assess your competency in the mathematics taught in the elementary school. The test is presented in seven sections. You may not want to take all of the sections at one time. This is your choice. The important thing is for you to do as well as you possibly can.

Assessment

SECTION ONE: SETS

A. Set Notation

1. The most correct way to represent a set whose elements are x, y, z is:
   a. (x, y, z)
   b. $\{x, y, z\}$
   c. $[x, y, z]$
   d. x, y, z

2. The statement "x is a member of set A" is represented in set notation by:

   a. $x \in A$ c. $x \rightarrow A$

   b. $x \ni A$ d. $\overset{\mathbf{A}}{x}$

3. The correct representation for the empty set is:

   a. $\{\varnothing\}$ c. [ ]

   b. π d. $\varnothing$

B. Subsets

1. If A is the set of all numbers and B is the set of all even numbers, then
   a. A is a subset of B.
   b. B is a subset of A.
   c. Neither is a subset of the other.
   d. They are the same set.
2. If $D \subset E$, then
   a. Every element of D is in E.
   b. D and E are equal sets.
   c. Every element of E is in D.
   d. There is an element of D not in E.
3. The set containing the elements 1, 2 has
   a. one subset   c. three subsets
   b. two subsets   d. four subsets

C. Set Operations

1. A is the set containing the elements 1, 2, 3, 4, 5. B is the set containing the elements 2, 4, 6. $A \cap B$ is:

   a. $\{1, 2, 3, 4, 5\}$ d. $\{2, 4\}$
   b. $\{2, 4, 6\}$ e. $\{1, 2, 3, 4, 5, 6\}$
   c. $\{1, 3, 5\}$
2. Using the same sets as in 1, $A \cup B$ is:

   a. $\{1, 2, 3, 4, 5, 6\}$ d. $\{2, 4, 6\}$
   b. $\{2, 4\}$ e. $\{1, 2, 3, 4, 5\}$
   c. $\{1, 3, 5\}$
3. If the Universe is the alphabet, and $A = \{a, b, c, d, e, f, g, h, i, x, y, z\}$, then the complement of A, or $\bar{A}$ is:

   a. $\{a, b, c, d, e, f, h, i, x, y, z\}$
   b. $\{a, b, c, d, e, f, g, h, i, j, k, l, m, n\}$
   c. $\{j, k, l, m, n, o, p, q, r, s, t, u, v, w\}$
   d. $\{b, d, f, h, x, z\}$

D. Basic Sets

1. The correct representation of the set of natural numbers is:
   a. $\{1, 2, 3, 4, \ldots\}$
   b. $\{0, 1, 2, 3, 4, \ldots\}$
   c. $\{\ldots -3, -2, -1, 0, 1, 2, 3, \ldots\}$
   d. $\{\ldots -3, \ldots -2\frac{1}{2}, \ldots -2, \ldots -\sqrt{2}, \ldots -1, \ldots -\frac{1}{2}, \ldots 0, \ldots \frac{1}{2}, \ldots 1, \ldots \sqrt{2}, \ldots 2, \ldots 2\frac{1}{2} \ldots\}$
   e. $\{\ldots -3, \ldots -2\frac{1}{2}, \ldots -2\frac{1}{4}, \ldots -2, \ldots -1\frac{3}{4}, \ldots -1, \ldots -\frac{1}{2}, \ldots 0, \ldots \frac{1}{2}, \ldots 1\}$

2. The correct representation of the set of integers is:
   a. $\{1, 2, 3, 4, \ldots\}$
   b. $\{0, 1, 2, 3, 4, \ldots\}$
   c. $\{\ldots -3, -2, -1, 0, 1, 2, 3, \ldots\}$
   d. $\{\ldots -3, \ldots -2\frac{1}{2}, \ldots -2, \ldots -\sqrt{2}, \ldots -1, \ldots -\frac{1}{2}, \ldots 0, \ldots \frac{1}{2}, \ldots 1, \ldots \sqrt{2}, \ldots 2, \ldots 2\frac{1}{2}, \ldots\}$
   e. $\{\ldots -3, \ldots -2\frac{1}{2}, \ldots -2\frac{1}{4}, \ldots -2, \ldots -1\frac{3}{4}, \ldots -1, \ldots -\frac{1}{2}, \ldots 0, \ldots \frac{1}{2}, \ldots 1\}$

3. The correct representation of the set of rationals is:
   a. $\{1, 2, 3, 4, \ldots\}$
   b. $\{0, 1, 2, 3, 4, \ldots\}$
   c. $\{\ldots -3, -2, -1, 0, 1, 2, 3, \ldots\}$
   d. $\{\ldots -3, \ldots -2\frac{1}{2}, \ldots -2, \ldots -\sqrt{2}, \ldots -1, \ldots -\frac{1}{2}, \ldots 0, \ldots \frac{1}{2}, \ldots 1, \ldots \sqrt{2}, \ldots 2, \ldots 2\frac{1}{2} \ldots\}$
   e. $\{\ldots -3, \ldots -2\frac{1}{2}, \ldots -2\frac{1}{4}, \ldots -2, \ldots -1\frac{3}{4}, \ldots -1, \ldots -\frac{1}{2}, \ldots 0, \ldots \frac{1}{2}, \ldots 1\}$

SECTION TWO: BASIC CONCEPTS

A. Natural Numbers

1. The successor of 3 is:
   a. 2   c. 3 and a very small fraction
   b. 4, 5, 6, ...   d. 4
2. The set $\{1, 2, 3, 4\}$ can *best* be described as:
   a. a finite set   c. a set of numbers
   b. an infinite set   d. a counting set
3. The sets $\{a, b, c\}$ and $\{d, e, f\}$ can *best* be described as:
   a. equivalent sets   c. alphabet sets
   b. equal sets   d. similar sets

B. Greater Than and Less Than

1. The mathematical sentence $a > b$ can *best* be verbally described as:
   - a. The number represented by a is on the number line to the left of the number represented by b.
   - b. The number represented by a is on the number line to the right of the number represented by b.
   - c. The set a has fewer members than the set b.
   - d. The set b has fewer members than the set a.
2. Sets which are equivalent to the set of natural numbers are sometimes called:
   - a. infinite
   - b. finite
   - c. countable
   - d. natural
3. The relationship between the sets $A = \{1, 2, 3, 4\}$ and $B = \{5, 6, 7, 8, 9\}$ might be described as:
   - a. $N(A) < N(B)$
   - b. $A < B$
   - c. $A > B$
   - d. $4 > 5$

C. Integers

1. If a profit of \$3 is represented by $^+3$, a loss of \$3 is represented by:
   - a. $+3$
   - b. -3
   - c. $^+3$
   - d. $^-3$
2. If x is negative $1 - x$ is
   - a. negative
   - b. 0
   - c. positive
   - d. cannot evaluate
3. $|-5|$ is:
   - a. -5
   - b. $\{-1, -2, -3, -4, -5\}$
   - c. $^-5$
   - d. 5
4. The points 9 and $^-9$ can be described mathematically as:
   - a. alike
   - b. negatives
   - c. opposites
   - d. equal

D. Rationals

1. If a and b are integers, a/b names a rational number provided that:
   - a. $a \neq 0$
   - b. $b \neq 0$
   - c. b is not negative
   - d. a is not negative
2. Which of the following represents an equivalence class?
   - a. $\{\frac{1}{2}, \frac{1}{4}, \frac{1}{6}, \frac{1}{8}, \frac{1}{10}, \ldots\}$
   - b. $\{\frac{1}{5}, \frac{2}{5}, \frac{3}{5}, \frac{4}{5}, \frac{5}{5}\}$
   - c. $\{\frac{1}{2}, \frac{2}{3}, \frac{3}{4}, \frac{4}{5}, \ldots\}$
   - d. $\{\frac{1}{2}, \frac{2}{4}, \frac{3}{6}, \frac{4}{8}, \frac{5}{10}, \frac{6}{12}, \ldots\}$

3. If a/b and c/d are rationals, $a/b = c/d$ if and only if:
    a. $ac = bd$ c. $ab = cd$
    b. $ad = bc$ d. $b/a = d/c$

E. Reals

1. Which of the following is a real number but not a rational?
    a. $\sqrt{9}$ b. $\sqrt{5}$ c. 0 d. $\sqrt{\frac{4}{9}}$
2. An irrational might be described as:
    a. a repeating decimal
    b. a non-repeating decimal
    c. a terminating decimal
    d. a square root
3. Which of the following is *not* a real number?
    a. $-\sqrt{2}$ b. 2 c. $\sqrt{-2}$ d. $\sqrt{2}$

F. Properties of Numbers

1. Which of the following describes the associative property of addition?
    a. $(a + b) + c = a + (b + c)$
    b. $a + b = b + a$
    c. $a(b + c) = ab + ac$
    d. $a + 0 = a$
2. Commutative property of multiplication?
    a. $(a \times b) \times c = a \times (b \times c)$
    b. $a \times b = b \times a$
    c. $a(b + c) = ab + ac$
    d. $a + 0 = a$
3. Distributive property?
    a. $(a \times b) \times c = a \times (b \times c)$
    b. $a \times b = b \times a$
    c. $a(b + c) = ab + ac$
    d. $a + 0 = a$
4. Additive property of 0?
    a. $(a \times b) \times c = a \times (b \times c)$
    b. $a \times b = b \times a$
    c. $a(b + c) = ab + ac$
    d. $a + 0 = a$
5. The identity element of multiplication is:
    a. 0 b. 1 c. $\times$ d. 2
6. Which of the following sets is closed under subtraction?
    a. $\{1, 2, 3, 4, \ldots\}$

b. $\{0, 1, 2, 3, 4, \ldots\}$
c. $\{1, \frac{1}{2}, \frac{1}{3}, \frac{1}{4}, \ldots\}$
d. $\{\ldots -3, -2, -1, 0, 1, 2, 3, \ldots\}$

SECTION THREE: OPERATIONS WITH NUMBERS

A. Whole Numbers

1. If $a + b = a + c$, then
   a. $a = b$ b. $a = c$ c. $a = a + b + c$ d. $b = c$
2. The answer to $8 - (5 - 2)$ is:
   a. 5   b. 1   c. 6   d. 2
3. 42×19 is:
   a. 798   b. 788   c. 888   d. 898
4. 2^4 means
   a. 4×4 c. $2 \times 2 \times 2 \times 2$
   b. 2×4 d. 32
5. $28 \div 7$ is:
   a. 4   b. $3\frac{6}{7}$ c. $\frac{1}{4}$ d. $1\frac{1}{7}$

B. Integers

1. $^-3 + {}^-7$ is:
   a. -4 b. 10   c. $^+4$ d. $^-10$
2. $^-3 + {}^+7$ is:
   a. $^-4$ b. 10   c. $^+4$ d. $^-10$
3. $^-3 - {}^+7$ is:
   a. $^-4$ b. 10   c. $^+4$ d. $^-10$
4. $^-3 - {}^-7$ is:
   a. -4 b. 10   c. $^+4$ d. $^-10$
5. $^+3 - {}^+7$ is:
   a. -4 b. 10   c. $^+4$ d. $^-10$
6. $^+3 - {}^-7$ is:
   a. $^-4$ b. 10   c. $^+4$ d. $^-10$
7. $^+3 \times {}^-7$ is:
   a. $^+21$ b. $^+4$ c. $^-4$ d. $^-21$
8. $^-3 \times {}^-7$ is:
   a. $^+21$ b. $^+10$ c. $^-10$ d. $^-21$
9. $^-8 \div {}^-2$ is:
   a. 16   b. $^+4$ c. $^-4$ d. $-\frac{1}{4}$
10. $^-8 \div {}^+2$ is:
    a. 16   b. $^+4$ c. $^-4$ d. $-\frac{1}{4}$

C. Rationals

1. $\frac{1}{3} + \frac{1}{3}$ is:
   a. $\frac{2}{6}$ b. $\frac{1}{9}$ c. $\frac{2}{3}$ d. $\frac{1}{3}$

2. $\frac{1}{3} + \frac{1}{6}$ is:
   a. $\frac{3}{6}$ or $\frac{1}{2}$ b. $\frac{2}{9}$ c. $\frac{1}{9}$ d. $\frac{2}{6}$

3. $\frac{3}{4} - \frac{1}{6}$ is:
   a. $\frac{2}{13}$ or $\frac{1}{6}$ b. $\frac{4}{2}$ or 2   c. $-\frac{2}{2}$ or -1 d. $\frac{7}{12}$

4. $\frac{1}{2} \times \frac{2}{7}$ is:
   a. $\frac{3}{14}$ b. $\frac{2}{14}$ or $\frac{1}{7}$ c. $\frac{7}{2}$ d. $\frac{7}{4}$

5. $\frac{1}{2} \div \frac{2}{7}$ is:
   a. $\frac{3}{14}$ b. $\frac{2}{14}$ or $\frac{1}{7}$ c. $\frac{7}{2}$ d. $\frac{7}{4}$

6. $\frac{68}{72}$ in lowest terms is:
   a. $\frac{34}{36}$ b. $1\frac{4}{72}$ or $1\frac{1}{18}$ c. $\frac{35}{36}$ d. $\frac{17}{18}$

D. Decimals

1. $1.4 + 0.2$ is:
   a. 3.4   b. 1.42   c. 1.6   d. 1.24

2. $1.4 - 0.37$ is:
   a. 1.03   b. 1.3   c. 1.17   d. -0.23

3. 1.4×0.3 is:
   a. 4.2   b. 0.42   c. 42   d. 1.12

4. $1.2 \div 3$ is:
   a. 4   b. 0.4   c. 0.04   d. $\frac{1}{4}$

5. $1.2 \div 0.3$ is:
   a. 4   b. 0.4   c. 0.04   d. $\frac{1}{4}$

6. $\frac{1}{5}$ as a decimal is:
   a. 0.1   b. 0.5   c. 0.02   d. 0.2

7. 0.4 as a fraction is:
   a. $\frac{1}{4}$ b. $\frac{2}{5}$ c. $\frac{4}{100}$ d. $\frac{4}{1}$

8. 0.2727 ... as a fraction is:
   a. $\frac{27}{100}$ b. $\frac{1}{27}$ c. $\frac{2727}{10,000}$ d. $\frac{27}{99}$

E. Ratio and Percent

1. There are 65 students in a class. 14 are girls.
   The ratio of girls to boys is:
   a. 14/65   b. 51/65   c. 14/51   d. 51/14

2. 2% means
   a. two portions out of one hundred
   b. two

  c. two pieces of a cent
  d. interest
3. What number is 6% of 150?
  a. 900   b. 3   c. 25   d. 9

F. Reals

1. $\sqrt{25}$ is:
  a. ± 5 b. ± 25 c. 5×5 d. 25
2. $\sqrt{45}$ simplified is:
  a. $3\sqrt{5}$ b. $5\sqrt{3}$ c. 6.5   d. $|15|$
3. $2\sqrt{3} - \sqrt{3}$ is:
  a. 2   b. $\sqrt{3}$ c. 3   d. 20
4. $\sqrt{3} \cdot \sqrt{4}$ is:
  a. $\sqrt{7}$ b. $\sqrt{1}$ c. $2\sqrt{3}$ d. 12

SECTION FOUR: GEOMETRY

1. A line is *best* described as
  a. infinite length
  b. no endpoints
  c. one dimension; length; goes to infinity
  d. a piece of string
2. The difference between a line segment and a ray is best described by
  a. one endpoint
  b. one can be measured, the other cannot
  c. a difference in length
  d. one has an arrow at the end
3. The correct notation for 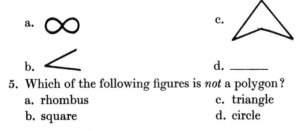 is

  a. $\angle BCA$ b. $\angle ACB$ c. $\angle ABC$ d. $\angle A$
4. Which of the following figures is a simple closed curve?

  a. ∞

  c. △

  b. <   d. _____
5. Which of the following figures is *not* a polygon?
  a. rhombus   c. triangle
  b. square   d. circle

6. A rectangle is *best* described as:
   a. a 4-sided polygon
   b. a square
   c. a parallelogram with right $\angle$s.
   d. a four-sided figure with rectified $\angle$s.
7. An obtuse $\angle$ has
   a. more than 90°, less than 180°
   b. more than 0°, less than 90°
   c. exactly 90°
   d. exactly 180°
8. If the base of a $\triangle$ is 6″, and its height is 3″, its area is
   a. 9″   c. 24 square inches
   b. 9 square inches   d. 3 square inches
9. If the length of a rectangle is 9″ and its width is 2″, its area is:
   a. 18 square inches   c. 18 inches
   b. 9 square inches   d. 11 square inches
10. If the radius of a circle is 3 inches, its area is:
    a. 9 square inches   c. 6π square inches
    b. 9 inches   d. 9π square inches
11. Which of the following is a correct statement of the Pythagorean Theorem?
    a. In a right $\triangle$, the square of the sides equals the square of the hypotenuse.
    b. The sum of the angles of the sides equals the angle of the hypotenuse.
    c. In a right triangle, the sum of the squares of the lengths of the sides equals the square of the length of the hypotenuse.
    d. The product of the legs of a right triangle equals the length of the hypotenuse.
12. How many inches are there in a yard?
    a. 12   b. 36   c. 24   d. 3
13. How many pints are there in a quart?
    a. $\frac{1}{2}$ b. 3   c. 4   d. 2
14. How many yards are there in a mile?
    a. 6,373   b. 5,280   c. 1,760   d. 5,180
15. How many decimeters in a meter?
    a. 3   b. 100   c. 10   d. 57

SECTION FIVE: NUMBER THEORY

1. Which of the following is a prime number?
   a. 7   b. 4   c. 1   d. 6

2. What is the prime factored form of 68?
    a. 68×1 c. $2^2 \times 17$
    b. 4×17 d. 8×17

3. What is the greatest common divisor of 28 and 35?
    a. 4   b. 980   c. 5   d. 7

4. What is the least common multiple of 28 and 35?
    a. 140   b. 980   c. 4   d. 7

5. If a divides $b + c$, and a divides b, then
    a. c divides a c. cannot tell if a divides c
    b. a divides c d. a cannot divide c

6. A quick test to see if a number is divisible by 3 is to—
    a. See if the last digit is a 3.
    b. See if the first digit is a 3.
    c. See if the sum of digits is a multiple of 3.
    d. See if the number is odd.

SECTION SIX: EQUATIONS

1. If $x + 2 = 8$, $x =$ _____
2. If $x/5 = 7$, $x =$ _____
3. If $2x = 9$, $x =$ _____
4. If $3x + 1 = 10$, $x =$ _____
5. If $x/2 - 6 = 11$, $x =$ _____
6. If $3(x + 7) = 9$, $x =$ _____

SECTION SEVEN: OTHER NUMERATION SYSTEMS

1. 17 expressed in Roman numerals is
    a. XIIIIIII   c. XVII
    b. IIIXXXL   d. XIIX

2. $7_{\text{base ten}}$ expressed in base five is:
    a. 12_{five} c. 11_{five}
    b. 12   d. 7_{five}

3. 372 in expanded notation is:
    a. $300 + 70 + 2$
    b. $(3 \times 10^2) + (7 \times 10^1) + (2 \times 10^0)$
    c. $(3 \times 10^2) \times (7 \times 10^1) \times (2 \times 10^0)$
    d. three hundred seventy-two

4. $34_{\text{base five}}$ expressed in base ten is:
    a. 34   b. 50   c. 19   d. 7

Answers and Activities

The answers to the problems in the preceding assessment are provided in the following sections. The answers to each section are followed by references where information on a particular problem type can be found. You will notice that the sets of answers are followed by a list of references. It is recommended if you miss two or three items out of three that you use the references, or similar material, to study that topic.

SECTION ONE: SETS

A. Set Notation

1. b   2. a   3. d

References

1. Peterson, John M. *Basic Concepts of Elementary Mathematics*. Boston: Prindle, Weber and Schmidt, Inc., pp. 21–22.
2. Lane, Bennie R. *Programmed Guide*. Boston: Prindle, Weber and Schmidt, Inc., 1971, 17D.
3. Hashisaki, Joseph, and John Peterson. *Theory of Arithmetic*. New York: John Wiley and Sons, 1964, pp. 20–25.
4. Matchett, Margaret, and David Snodes. *Modern Elementary Mathematics*. Boston: Prindle, Weber and Schmidt, 1972, pp. 1–7.

B. Subsets

1. b   2. a   3. d

References

1. 1. Peterson, p. 27;   2. Lane, 24C;   3. Hashisaki, pp. 24–28;   4. Matchet, pp. 9–15.

C. Set Operations

1. d   2. a   3. c

References

1. Peterson, pp. 29–36;   2. Lane, 32C, 25D;   3. Hashisaki, pp. 29–31;
4. Matchett, pp. 17–23.

D. Basic Sets

1. a   2. c   3. e

References

1. Peterson, pp. 49, 108, 163, 282–89;   2. Lane, 42B, 81D, 121B, 204B, 208B, 208C;   3. Hashisaki, pp. 81, 112, 151, 193;   4. Matchett, pp. 54, 159, 279, 405.

SECTION TWO: BASIC CONCEPTS

A. Natural Numbers

1. d   2. a and d   3. a

References

4. Matchett, pp. 45–49.

B. Greater Than and Less Than

1. b   2. a   3. a

References

1. Peterson, pp. 68–69;   2. Lane, 57B;   4. Matchet, p. 57.

C. Integers

1. d   2. c   3. d   4. c

References

1. Peterson, pp. 107–10;   2. Lane, 81B;   3. Hashisaki, pp. 112–19;   4. Matchett, pp. 159–61.

D. Rationals

1. b   2. d   3. b

References

1. Peterson, pp. 163–64;   2. Lane, 116C, 121B;   3. Hashisaki, pp. 151–59;   4. Matchett, pp. 279, 318.

25

E. Reals

1. b   2. b   3. c

References

1. Peterson, p. 289;   2. Lane, 166B;   3. Hashisaki, Chapter 8;   4. Matchett, pp. 405–11.

F. Properties of Numbers

1. a   2. b   3. c   4. d   5. b   6. d

References

4. Matchett, pp. 71, 103, 110.

SECTION THREE: OPERATIONS WITH NUMBERS

A. Whole Numbers

1. d   2. a   3. a   4. c   5. a

References

1. Peterson, Chapter 3;   2. Lane, 44D, 48B, 52B;   3. Hashisaki, Chapter 5; 4. Matchett, pp. 65–103.

B. Integers

1. d   2. c   3. d   4. c   5. a   6. b   7. d   8. a   9. b   10. c

References

1. Peterson, chapter 5;   2. Lane, 83C, 85C, 86D, 92C;   3. Hashisaki, Chapter 6;   4. Matchett, Chapter 6.

C. Rationals

1. c   2. a   3. d   4. b   5. d   6. d

References

1. Peterson, Chapter 7;   2. Lane, 127B, 126D, 135C;   3. Hashisaki, Chapter 7;   4. Matchett, Chapter 9.

D. Decimals

1. c   2. a   3. b   4. b   5. a   6. d   7. b   8. d

References

1. Peterson, Chapter 9;   2. Lane, 156D, 163B, 164C;   3. Hashisaki, pp. 200–17;   4. Matchett, pp. 331–36.

E. Ratio and Percent

1. c   2. a   3. d

References

4. Matchett, pp. 357–65.

F. Reals

1. a   2. a   3. b   4. c

References

1. Peterson, pp. 289–92;   2. Lane, 208C;   3. Hashisaki, Chapter 8;   4. Matchett, p. 414.

SECTION FOUR: GEOMETRY

1. c   2. a   3. c   4. c   5. d   6. c   7. a   8. b   9. a   10. d
11. c   12. b   13. d   14. c   15. c

References

1. Peterson, Chapter 10;   2. Lane, 172C, 173C, 178C, 183D, 193C;   3. Hashisaki, Chapter 9;   4. Matchet, Chapters 8, 11.

SECTION FIVE: NUMBER THEORY

1. a   2. c   3. d   4. a   5. b   6. c

References

1. Peterson, Chapter 6;   2. Lane, 94D, 97D, 105B, 109B, 103D, 113B;   4. Matchett, Chapter 7.

SECTION SIX: EQUATIONS

1. 6   2. 35   3. $4\frac{1}{2}$ 4. 3   5. 34   6. -4

References

1. Peterson, Chapters 3, 5, 7, pp. 289–92;   2. Lane, 44D, 48B, 52B, 83C, 85C, 86D, 92C, 127B, 126D, 135C, 156D, 163B, 164C, 208C;   3. Hashisaki, Chapters 5, 6, 7, 8, pp. 200–17;   4. Matchett, Chapters 6, 9; pp. 65–103, 331–36, 357–65, 414.

SECTION SEVEN: OTHER NUMERATION SYSTEMS

1. c   2. a   3. b   4. c

References

1. Peterson, Chapter 4;   2. Lane, 64C, 64D, 65B, 70B;   3. Hashisaki, Chapter 4;   Matchett, Chapter 5.

Instructional Content for Mathematics Programs in Elementary Schools

The basic concepts of mathematics taught in the elementary school are sequenced in such a way that children study them in a logical order. Being familiar with this content and its sequence and age placement is important for the teacher of elementary school mathematics.

Successfully completing Component I indicates that your knowledge of the mathematical content is adequate. The purpose of this component is to provide you with a means of learning the scope and sequence of mathematics programs in elementary schools.

An investigation of several elementary school mathematics programs will show that there is no one scope and sequence. However, most programs are more alike than they are different. Therefore, it is possible to know, in general, what is being taught at each grade level or age level in the program.

Component II has three objectives. Each objective is followed by (a) instructional material, (b) a list of learning activities, and (c) a self-assessment exercise. This format will also be used in the remaining components.

IIA

> List the mathematics content taught at a given grade level or age level.

This objective concerns the scope (what is taught) and the sequence (when and in what order is it taught) of the elementary school mathematics program. The material which follows will provide an overview of the concepts that are introduced at each grade level. It should be noted that the

26

divisions within each grade level correspond to those on the self-assessment in Component I.

IIA.1. Instructional Material

FIRST GRADE

Sets: The idea of a set and a number corresponding to each set is developed. The child learns to compare sets, developing the ideas of more than, fewer than, one more than, one less than, equivalent sets, ordering sets, and the empty sets. Presentation of simple set operations, such as joining sets, taking sets away, separating sets into sets with the same number of members, and the concept of $\frac{1}{2}$ of and $\frac{1}{4}$ of a set is at this level.

Basic Concepts: At this level, the emphasis is on the set of natural numbers. The child learns to write numerals from 1 to 99, and to recognize word names for the numbers one through ten. Along with this there should be some idea of different names for the same number, and the ability to group by tens. There is emphasis on the meaning of zero, the property of zero for addition, the associative property of addition, the ordinal numbers, and order on a number line for the numbers 0 through 99.

Operations with Numbers: The child learns basic addition facts through 12 and is able to add and subtract on a number line. The use of zero in addition and subtraction is mastered, along with the ability to add and subtract in both horizontal and vertical forms. Also, the child can illustrate the relationship between addition and subtraction.

Geometry and Measurement: At this level, the circle, triangle, rectangle, and square are introduced, and a distinction made between the inside and outside of a figure. The child learns to use a ruler to the nearest inch and to decide which of a set of lengths is the longest. The commonly used measures of liquid and weight—pints, quarts, and pounds—are discussed, along with the measures of time—hour and half-hour. With respect to money, the student is expected to learn the value of a penny, a nickel, and a dime, and to be able to exchange one for its count value in another (example, exchange a nickel for five pennies).

Equations and Problem Solving: The symbols $+$, $-$ and $=$ are introduced, along with parentheses, and their mathematical use. The child learns to write addition and subtraction sentences and to reverse them. He learns to write number sentences for simple problems (pictured or read) and to solve for the correct addend.

SECOND GRADE

Sets: The concept of $\frac{1}{3}$ of a set is introduced and the child compares sets of money.

Basic Concepts: The child learns to group by twos and fives, as well as tens. He masters the ability to read and write numerals from 0 to 999, and thus, place value to the hundreds place. Along with this is the concept of one hundred and the ordering of numbers from 0 to 1,000. The meaning of multiplication is discussed, along with the role of zero in multiplication. The child is expected to know the meaning of the terms factor and product.

Operations with Numbers: Still in the realm of whole numbers, addition problems to the level of three addends, each a two-digit numeral, are covered. The child is able to add with four or more addends and can add and subtract hundreds, tens, and ones, regrouping if necessary. He can check both addition and subtraction, and has knowledge of the multiplication facts through 5. There is some readiness for division.

Geometry and Measurement: The child learns to identify sides, corners, inside, and outside of a figure, and can draw a line segment and identify its endpoints. The concept of "betweenness" is presented, as well as the concept of yearly time measured in months, weeks, and days. The knowledge of daily time is expanded to include the quarter-hours and five-minute intervals. With respect to money, the child is taught the value of a half-dollar, a quarter, and the ability to determine the value of sets of coins less than one dollar. The measurement of "foot" and "centimeter" are introduced, and the child learns to measure to the nearest $\frac{1}{2}$ inch. He also is taught how to use scales for simple weighings and how to read a thermometer. The liquid measurements of cup, gallon, and half-gallon are introduced, along with the measuring idea of dozen and half dozen.

Equations and Problem Solving: The symbols > and < are introduced. The child learns to write simple multiplication sentences and to choose the correct number sentence to fit a given problem.

THIRD GRADE

Sets: The connection between zero and the number of the empty set is made. The concepts of joining and separating sets in multiplication and division are introduced, as well as the concept of equivalent fractional portions of sets.

Basic Concepts: The meaning of zero and the concept of inequalities are amplified. The concept of a fraction as a part of a whole is introduced, along with expanded notation for a numeral. The child learns to write word names for all numbers and place value through the hundred thousands. He also learns to round numbers to the nearest hundred. The following properties are presented: commutative property of addition and multiplication, associative property of multiplication, identity element of multiplication, distributive property of multiplication over addition.

Operations with Numbers: Again, all operations are with the whole numbers. The concept of estimation is introduced, as well as the relationship between division and fractions. The child learns to add and subtract numbers to the thousands place and learns to multiply and divide all combinations of the factors from 1 to 9. He also learns to relate multiplication to division and division to related subtraction. Multiplication with three factors is mastered, as well as the ability to multiply hundreds with regrouping. Division symbolism is presented and the child learns to divide hundreds, tens, and ones, and to handle remainders.

Geometry and Measurements: The concepts of parallel lines and symmetry are introduced, as well as that of perimeter of a geometric figure. The terms unit of measure, yard, meter, minute, boiling point, and freezing point are presented and discussed. The child learns to measure to the nearest quarter inch and to the nearest centimeter, and to compare linear and metric measures. He also learns to identify the radius, diameter, and circumference of a circle.

Equations and Problem Solving: The interpretations of charts and graphs are presented, along with the procedure for comparing simple fractions. The child learns to discard excess information in problems and to realize when too little information is offered. He also, at this level, acquires the ability to solve problems involving any concept he has studied.

FOURTH GRADE

Sets: Formal presentation of the set of whole numbers as well as the set of natural numbers occurs here, as well as the correct notational form for finite and infinite sets.

Basic Concepts: The terms numerator and denominator are presented, along with the inability to divide by zero in our number system. All properties studied so far are extended for the set of fractions. The child learns the cardinal and the ordinal use of a number, and how to distinguish an even from an odd number. He also learns to order fractions on the number line and acquires the ability to mark off numerals by periods.

Other Bases: The Egyptian and Roman number systems are introduced, along with simple computation in both.

Operations with Numbers: In the realm of whole numbers, the emphasis is on division—division related to subtraction, division with money, estimation and partial quotient, and checking division. In the realm of non-zero rationals, the recognition of fractions with like denominators whose sum is greater than one. The child learns the procedure to decide if two fractional numbers are equivalent.

Geometry and Measurement: Some of the new terms introduced and discussed at this level are points, paths, rays, intersections, angles, symmetry, reflections, rotations, base, vertex, cone, perpendicular segments, diagonals, rectangular boxes, miles, kilometers, grams, kilograms, fathoms, and tons. Correct notation for all geometric figures studied so far is presented. The different types of angles and triangles are demonstrated. The child learns to compare geometric shapes and to use a compass to draw circles. He can measure to the nearest $\frac{1}{8}$ inch. The concept of money both as parts of a dollar and as decimals is presented. By this level, the child should be able to make change. And he should be able to compute time in terms of hours, minutes, seconds, A.M., P.M., decade, score, and century.

Equations and Problem Solving: The child learns to interpret and to solve problems concerning picture and bar graphs. He learns to solve simple two-step problems and to compute averages.

FIFTH GRADE

Sets: The set of integers is formally introduced. The student learns to name sets of multiples, sets of ordered pairs, and sets according to some given rule (example: Describe a set beginning with 3 and increasing by 2 each time).

Basic Concepts: The concept of reciprocal of a number is introduced, as well as the use of exponential notation. All the properties previously studied are applied to the set of integers. Zero is again discussed and presented as neither positive nor negative. The child learns what a least common denominator is. He should have a good understanding of our number system as the Hindu-Arabic system, based on ten, and be able to write word names for numbers through billions. He learns to organize data and make simple tables and to round numbers to the nearest 1,000.

Other Bases: The student learns to perform basic computation in both base five and the Roman Number System.

Number Theory: The idea of prime and composite numbers is introduced, and the Sieve of Erathosthenes is presented. The child learns to compute the least common multiple and the greatest common factor.

Operations with Numbers: The use of the abacus in addition is presented. Where integers are concerned, the child learns to perform simple addition. Where rationals are concerned, the child learns to compare fractions and decimals, choosing the larger. He can perform addition, subtraction, and multiplication of decimals. He learns to divide a whole number by a fraction and to handle a fractional answer. Likewise, in whole number division, he learns to express the remainders as fractions. Where whole numbers are concerned, he can factor any number into primes or multiply any number. He can perform short form division. The role of zero and of one in division is presented here.

Geometry and Measurement: The description of a rhombus, a parellelogram, a trapezoid, a millimeter, a gram, a kilogram, a liter, a fluid ounce, and of the standard units of area and volume (square and cubic) are introduced.

The child learns to identify basic three-dimensional figures, pointing out edges and faces. He learns to identify simple closed figures and congruent figures. He learns to draw perpendiculars and to measure to the nearest $\frac{1}{16}$ of an inch. Computation of the area of a right triangle, the area of a rectangle, and the circumference of a circle are taught here. The child also learns to add and subtract all known measures, making any necessary conversions.

Equations and Problem Solving: Letters as variables are introduced. The child learns to solve simple equations to form true sentences. He can determine the correct operation in writing a number sentence for a verbal problem and learns to write number sentences for two-step problems involving any concept previously discussed.

SIXTH GRADE

Sets: The precedure for computing the mean, median, and mode of sets of numbers is presented. The student learns to set up replacement sets, solution sets, sets of factors and multiples, sets of ordered pairs, and sets of equivalent numbers.

Basic Concepts: The derivation of Pi is presented. The meaning of powers and exponents is discussed, along with scientific notation. The student learns to recognize repeating decimal numerals.

Other Bases: The child learns the basis of the Egyptian numeration system and learns to perform basic computations in base five, six, seven, and eight.

Operations with Numbers: Percent, ratio, and simple interest are presented. Also, explanations of algorithms for addition, subtraction, multiplication, and division of whole numbers and rationals are presented. The student learns to subtract integers and to perform all four basic operations upon fractions with speed and accuracy. He also learns to relate fractional and decimal numerals, changing from one to the other.

Geometry and Measurement: The three-dimensional figures, rectangular prism, triangular prism, sphere, cone, and cylinder, are presented and discussed. Latitude and longitude of a position are also presented. The child learns to find the perimeter of any plane figure and the volume of rectangular prism and right triangular prisms. He learns to use a protractor and to read scale drawings and maps.

Equations and Problem Solving: The child learns to write a verbal sentence to fit a verbal problem and learns to solve any problem involving any concept taught up to now.

IIA.2. Learning Activities

   a. Examine an elementary school mathematics textbook series. These books can usually be obtained from a local school or the library.

b. Examine a curriculum guide for elementary school mathematics. Most schools will have a curriculum guide for their teachers.

c. Talk with an elementary school teacher about the mathematics that is taught in a particular grade level.

d. Read Chapter 2: "Scope, Sequence, Aims and Trends" in *Teaching Elementary School Mathematics for Understanding.*

e. Read pages 3–6 in *Teaching Elementary School Mathematics: What Research Says to the Teacher.*

f. Read pages 1–31 in *Elementary School Mathematics: A Guide to Current Research.*

g. Read pages 7–24 in *Discovering Meanings in Elementary School Mathematics.*

IIA.3. Self-assessment

a. Select a grade level and list all the mathematical concepts that are taught at that level. Compare your list with an elementary school text.

b. Ask someone to prepare a list of ten mathematical concepts that are taught in the elementary school. Identify the grade level in which each of the ten is introduced. Compare your answers with a textbook series.

IIB

> Identify the prerequisite mathematical concepts and/or skills for a given concept and/or skill.

Solving a mathematical problem may require any number of specific concepts and/or skills. Teachers should know the concepts and/or skills required for any given problem. This knowledge enables the teacher to analyze pupil errors and thus design instructional sequences which help the learner with specific difficulties.

IIB.1. Instructional Materials

To illustrate this competency, consider a subtraction problem involving two 2-digit numerals where no regrouping is required. For example, $38 - 17 = \Box$. The concepts and/or skills involved are:

1. The meaning of subtraction.
2. The addition and/or subtraction facts.
3. An understanding of place value.

IIB.2. Learning Activities

a. Select a concept area in mathematics (e.g., addition of whole numbers) and trace its development through a series of elementary school texts.
b. Work pages 186–209 and 243–75 in *Teaching Elementary School Mathematics.*
c. Examine an elementary school level programmed textbook (e.g., *Lessons for Self Instruction in Basic Skills* by California Test Bureau [a division of McGraw-Hill Book Company]) and determine the sequence of presentation.
d. Examine a slide series (e.g., *Harbrace Mathematics Instructional Slides* by Harcourt Brace Jovanovich, Incorporated) and determine the sequence of presentation.

IIB.3. Self-assessment

a. List the concepts and/or skills needed to add three 3-digit numerals where regrouping is involved. For example, $256 + 324 + 173 = \square$. Compare your list with another person's list.
b. List the concepts and/or skills needed to determine the area of a rectangle. Compare your list with another person's list.

IIC

> Illustrate two or more algorithms for each arithmetic operation with whole numbers and rational numbers.

An algorithm is a process or procedure for solving a problem and recording the computations. For example, in the United States the most common algorithm for solving $54 - 36 = \square$ is: 4 take away 6. Not enough in the one's place. Regroup one 10 as ones. 14 take away 6 equals 8. 4 take away 3 equals 1. The answer is $54 - 36$ is 18. This is usually recorded as follows:

A	B	C	D
5 4	$4\,\cancel{5}^1 4$	$4\,\cancel{5}^1 4$	$4\,\cancel{5}^1 4$
− 3 6	− 3 6	− 3 6	− 3 6
		8	1 8

IIC.1. Instructional Materials

The following algorithms differ from those that are normally taught in the schools. They are not an exhaustive listing.

Trachtenburg Addition

```
3 5 6      (1)  4 + 8 = 12
4 5 8√     (2)  12 exceeds 11 by 1.
+ 3 3 4    (3)  Record a √ for the 11.
───────    (4)  1 + 6 = 7
    7
```

```
1 5√6      (5)  3 + 5 = 8
4 5 8√     (6)  8 + 5 = 13
3 3 4      (7)  13 exceeds 11 by 2.
─────      (8)  Record a √ for the 11.
  2 7
```

```
1 5√6      (9)   3 + 4 = 7
4 5 8√     (10)  7 + 1 = 8
3 3 4      (11)  There is one √ in the ones place: record same.
─────      (12)  There is one √ in the tens place: record same.
8 2 7      (13)  7 + 1 = 8
  1 1      (14)  2 + 1 + 1 = 4
9 4 8      (15)  8 + 1 = 9
```

Scratch Subtraction

$^1{\not7}$ 3 5 9   (1) $7 - 6 = 1$. Scratch 7, 6 and put 1 above the 7.
$- {\not6}$ 4 1 5

$^1{\not7}^9{\not3}$ 5 9   (2) $13 - 4$ is 9. Scratch 1, 3, 4 and put 9 above 3.
$- {\not6} {\not4}$ 1 5

$^1{\not7}^9{\not3}^4{\not5}$ 9   (3) $95 - 1 = 94$. Scratch 9, 5, 1, putting 9 above the
$- {\not6}$ 4 ${\not1}$ 5   other 9, 4 above 5.

$^1{\not7}^9{\not3}^4{\not5}{\not9}$ (4) $49 - 5 = 44$. Scratch 4, 9, and 5, putting 4 above
$- {\not6}$ 4 ${\not1}$ ${\not5}$ the 4, and 4 above the 9.

                                   (5) Read your answer, 944, at the top, from the
                                        "unscratched" numbers.

IIC.2. Learning Activities

a. Examine an elementary mathematics textbook series and determine what algorithms are being taught.

b. Read pages 109–18, 139–52 and 200–08 in *Teaching Elementary School Mathematics for Understanding.*

c. Read page 21 in *Teaching Elementary School Mathematics: What Research Says to the Teacher.*

d. Read pages 133–52, 182–204 and 222–69 in *Discovering Meanings in Elementary School Mathematics.*

e. Read pages 253–57 in *The Arithmetic Teacher,* April, 1969.

IIC.3. Self-assessment

Solve the following using two different algorithms for each problem:

a.
$$346$$
$$756$$
$$488$$
$$+763$$

c.
$$325$$
$$\times\ 73$$

e. $\frac{1}{6} + \frac{3}{4} + \frac{2}{3} =$

g. $2\frac{2}{5} \times 3\frac{7}{10} =$

b.
$$7642$$
$$-4563$$

d. $26\overline{)7896}$

f. $3\frac{2}{3} - 1\frac{3}{4} =$

h. $\frac{3}{4} \div \frac{2}{3} =$

Behavioral Approaches in Mathematics Education

Teaching and learning have sometimes been characterized as two sides of the same coin. While recognizing the inter-relatedness of the two, we take the position that they are not the same phenomena viewed from two perspectives—that of the learner and the instructor. Teaching can take place without learning. Consider the example of the teacher of 30 children, 5 of whom do not demonstrate that they have learned, and 25 who do. Has the instructor taught or not? Has he taught 25/30 so that the degree of "teaching" corresponds with the success of instruction? Defining teaching by specifying the results of teaching is to do disservice to the instructor. But what we are more concerned with is not simply teaching, but *successful* teaching; and this can be defined in pupil outcome terminology. The former implies that the instructor *intended* to bring about change through stipulated instructional processes, while the latter specifies that such instruction led to change in pupils. Just as not all teaching leads to learning, not all learning is derived from teaching. The child touches a hot stove, is burned, and never touches it again. One cannot assume that the stove is a teacher, nor that it "taught" the child something. *There was no intent;* the stove did not initiate action designed to bring about change in the child's behavior.

On several occasions during the past six decades, educators have attempted to draw specific instructional strategies from theories of learning. Each time the results have been less than spectacular. Yet the relationship does exist, and drawing upon a sound research base in the behavioral sciences can facilitate mathematics instruction in the elementary classroom. This component is not meant to be comprehensive; indeed it does not begin to summarize the scope of several excellent texts and the scholarly activities of many pyschologists, sociologists, cultural economists, anthropologists, cultural geographers, and other behavioral scientists. It does, however, direct the reader's attention to several very salient concepts which contribute to more effective mathematics education. The work of three learning theorists

(Jean Piaget, Robert Gagné, and Jerome Bruner) are described, contrasted, and implications for mathematics education drawn in this component. Several societal factors of direct import to mathematics instruction are sketched; and readings which amplify these are identified. Specifically, in this component the objectives are:

IIIA

> Describe developmental stages as identified by Piaget.
>
> Describe the eight levels of learning as specified by Robert Gagné.
>
> Compare and contrast the theories of Gagné and Bruner.
>
> Discuss implications of psychological theories for mathematics education, and
>
> Discuss the implications of societal factors for mathematics learning.

IIIA.1. Instructional Materials

JEAN PIAGET

During the past decade American psychologists and educators have suddenly discovered a Swiss psychologist whose five decades of research and writings has led to some of the most consequential findings. Interviewing thousands of children and asking them to perform series of tasks led Jean Piaget to describe a prescribed sequence of developmental stages through which all children seem to pass.

Too often teachers assume that children can and do learn in the same ways as adults. Piaget's work has proven this to be false; it appears there are vast differences between the way adults and children learn concepts.

Piaget studied the thought processes of children through a series of experiments which revealed the manner in which children conceptualize the invariance of quantitative properties such as weight and volume. In a classic experiment he pours liquid into two glasses of equal size and shape. After the child affirms that the amount is equal, the contents of one glass is poured into a wide flat dish. Before a certain age, children indicate that one container or the other now has more liquid (as though the shape of the container determined the amount). But after he is able to "conserve" quantity, as Piaget defines the phenomenon, the child recognizes that container shape does not affect the amount of the liquid.

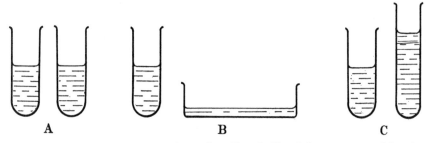

A   B   C

Another experiment employs clay. Two balls of clay are agreed by the child to be equal in size. One ball is then successively patted out into a flat patty, rolled into cylindrical shape, and broken into several smaller pieces; after each operation the child is asked to decide which is larger. After he has reached the conservation stage, the child recognizes that shape has no effect on the mass of clay.

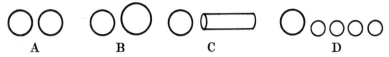

A   B   C   D

These conservation experiments provide an excellent indicator of the child's intellectual development. In another experiment utilizing more advanced concepts, a child first associates the number 10 with a set of ten objects. Then the experimenter reshapes the pile of objects, divides it into two or more piles, or rearranges it in any one of a number of ways. After each operation he asks the question, "Now how many objects are there?" If the child, without recounting the objects, answers ten, then it may be concluded that he conserves the concept of tenness.

This is important to understanding addition. The child must comprehend that a set of seven and a set of three objects, when joined together, total ten objects; that ten other objects can be placed in one-to-one correspondence with these ten; and that 7 + 3 and 10 are really two names for the same number.

Children develop through a series of continuous transformations of thought processes. According to Piaget, a developmental stage is a period of months or years during which changes take place. Because of the continuity of change, specific delineation of stages is often difficult. While the sequence of stages through which children pass remains constant, the ages at which children complete various stages is not. Piaget identified four primary stages of development: sensorimotor, preoperational thought, concrete operations, and formal operations.

Sensorimotor intelligence develops from birth to the appearance of language; that is, until about two years of age. This stage is characterized by the progressive acquisition of the permanence of an object. By the end of this period, he has acquired what Piaget calls "object permanency"; the child no longer acts as if objects disappear completely once they are out of his sight.

By the end of the first month of life, not only can the child perceive relatively minor differences in the object he views, but he shows a preference for complex patterns over simple stimuli. For example, when shown two rectangular frames of equivalent size, but one with a cross-hatch design on its interior, the young child will make definite movements toward the more complex rectangle. During the later part of the sensorimotor intelligence stage, the child becomes aware of "self-other," and language begins to appear.

The second stage, *Preoperational Thought*, extends from approximately two years of age to six or seven years. Thought at this stage is based largely on perception; and usually only one aspect, dimension, or relation is considered in making judgments. In the experiment with liquids in various shaped bottles, the child at this stage will consider only height, for example, in making his decision—thus neglecting other dimensions.

Mental manipulation at this stage merely represents what the child would actually be doing physically with objects. As he progresses through this stage, he is increasingly able to internalize symbols and to discriminate between words and the concrete objects they represent.

Late in the preoperational stage the child develops the ability to classify. Sets of objects which include three elements are equated with the number 3. He is also able to order objects by size, from smallest to largest. However, he is not yet able to synthesize these two operations into a single reversible operation.

In the third stage, *Concrete Operations*, the child considers two or three dimensions simultaneously instead of successively. This stage lasts from six or seven to eleven or twelve years of age. He no longer centers his attention on a particular aspect of an action and is able to mentally reverse his action. No longer would he be confused by the change in container size or the different shapes of clay.

Piaget defines operation as an action of the child which (1) can be internalized symbolically, (2) is reversible, and (3) is never isolated. During the concrete operation stage, the child develops conservation of concepts in this order—substance, weight, and volume.

About the age of seven the concrete-operations child develops an interest in playing games involving rules and is capable of cooperative endeavor with others. Mathematical games become interesting to him.

Beginning at about eleven or twelve years of age the child develops abstract thought patterns and enters the fourth stage, *Formal Operations*.

Reasoning is accomplished using symbols without the necessity of perception. In contrast to the child whose thought is still dependent upon manipulation of concrete objects, the adolescent is capable of forming hypotheses and deducing all the possible consequences from them. These new operational abilities open unlimited possibilities for him to participate in the development of mathematics.

The most important general property of formal operational thought, the one from which Piaget derives all others, concerns the real versus the possible. When approaching a new problem, the child begins by formulating all the possibilities and then determining which ones in fact do hold true through experimentation and logical analysis.

Many educators have turned to Piaget's theory to seek help for new pedagogical approaches. His theories and experiments, however, are not directly convertible into teaching strategies and materials. While a child's reaction to a Piagetian task will enable a well trained researcher to determine the child's intellectual level, these same tasks or experiments will not improve his competencies if directly taught to the child. While his experiments should not be taught in the elementary school, the results of his experimentation provide viable and important new insights for those designing mathematics curricula and for those teaching boys and girls.

Robert M. Gagné

A second learning theorist, Robert Gagné, has influenced the structure and sequence of mathematics instruction in the United States. For him, observable changes in human behavior comprise the only criteria for inferring that learning has occurred. In instruction, desired learnings or objectives are stated specifically and behaviorally. When the individual is able to perform certain specific functions under specified conditions (such as solving a problem in arithmetic or identifying basic assumptions in a geometric problem), he has demonstrated learning or a "capability." This capability can be conceived of as a terminal behavior with enabling behaviors which are necessary prerequisites. In Figure 1, prerequisite capabilities 1, 2, 3, 4, and 5 are necessary before the individual can master capability 6. After the student has mastered capabilities 1 and 2, likewise, he is ready to develop capability 4.

Specifying these prerequisites leads to identifying levels or types of learning. Gagné has specified eight types of learning: problem solving, rule learning, concept learning, discrimination learning, verbal association, chaining, stimulus-response learning, and signal learning. If the mathematics capability desired, for example, is problem solving, then the learner must first develop capabilities for rule learning and concept learning. These in turn require discrimination learning and signal learning. Thus, it is possible to take a specified behavior which the student is to learn and through analysis complete a map of the necessary prerequisites. The resulting pattern identifies precisely what must be taught and the sequence. This model is appropriate for designing programmed or highly structured materials. After prerequisities are identified, an instructor or program designer may sequence them into linear steps and a tight teaching program.

The eight types of learning identified by Gagné are described in the following paragraphs:[1]

Signal Learning. The individual acquires a conditioned response to a given signal. Signal learning responses are diffuse, emotional, and the learning is involuntary. Pavlov studied such learning in great detail. Salivation of a dog upon hearing food poured in his feeding dish or the withdrawal of a hand upon sight of a hot object are two examples of conditioned responses.

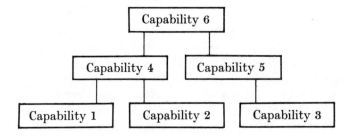

Figure 1. Pyramid of Capabilities

Stimulus-Response Learning. Whereas the responses from signal learning are diffuse and emotional, the responses in stimulus-response learning (often called operant conditioning) are fairly precise physical movements. Training a dog to sit, stay, or lie down is an example of stimulus-response learning. At first the trainer may use a leash, but later the verbal commands are all that is necessary.

Chaining. Frequently called skill learning, in chaining the person links together two or more units of stimulus-response learning. Limited to non-verbal sequences, chaining requires proper sequence of stimulus-response units. The elementary school child acquires many such chains: running, writing, catching, or throwing.

Verbal Association. This type is a form of chaining, but the links are verbal units. The simplest verbal association is that of naming an object,

[1]Robert M. Gagné, *The Conditions of Learning*, second edition (New York: Holt, Rinehart and Winston, Inc., 1970).

which involves a chain of two links: observing an object and identifying it and/or articulating the proper name.

Multiple Discrimination. The student learns different responses or stimuli which identify something but which might be confused with other similar things or phenomena. Identifying the make and model of automobiles or the names of children in a classroom are examples of multiple discrimination learning. In each case the learner must associate each individual or automobile model with its distinctive appearance and correct name, and with no other name.

Concept learning. Individuals learn concepts by responding to stimuli in terms of abstract characteristics like position, shape, color, and number as opposed to concrete physical properties. With experience, the concept of "chair" may refer to chairs which are padded, straight-backed, rocking chairs, or of various colors, of various sizes, with or without arms. Concepts have concrete references even though they are learned with the use of language.

Principle Learning. Learning principles requires one to relate two or more concepts. Principles are in effect chains of concepts.

Problem Solving. In the set of events called problem solving, individuals use principles to achieve some goal. In the process of achieving this goal, however, one becomes capable of new performances using his new knowledge. What is learned, according to Gagné, is a higher order principle: the combined product of two or more lower order principles.

JEROME BRUNER

While Robert Gagné's emphasis is primarily on the *product* of learning, Jerome Bruner emphasizes the *process* of learning.[2] Bruner summarizes his psychology of learning in these words:

"... to instruct someone in these disciplines is not a matter of getting him to commit the results in mind; rather, it is to teach him to participate in the process that makes possible the establishment of knowledge. We teach a subject, not to produce little living libraries from the subject, but rather to get a student to think mathematically for himself, to consider matters as a historian does, to take part in the process of knowledge-getting. Knowing is a process, not a product."[3]

For Gagné, the crucial question is, "*What* do you want the child to know?" For Bruner, it seems to be, "*How* do you want the child to know?" Gagné

[2]Adapted from Lee S. Shulman, "Perspectives on the Psychology of Learning and the Teaching of Mathematics," in W. Robert Houston, editor, *Improving Mathematics Education for Elementary School Teachers* (East Lansing, Michigan: Michigan State University, 1968), pp. 23–37.

[3]Jerome Bruner, *Toward a Theory of Instruction* (Cambridge, Massachusetts: Harvard University Press, 1966).

emphasizes *learning*, whether it is by discovery, by review, or by practice. But for Bruner the emphasis is on learning by *discovery*. It is the method of learning which is significant.

Bruner, like Piaget, emphasizes the child as a developing organism. Each child passes through stages which are biologically determined and age-related. Instruction is primarily dependent upon the level which the student has reached.

Curriculum Implications

Implications for the curriculum growing from the learning theories of Gagné and Bruner lead to programs which are quite different. Gagné emphasizes problem solving as the highest level of learning with lower levels prerequisite to it. For him, the appropriate sequence in learning is from these lower levels toward problem solving. The teacher begins with simple mathematical ideas, relates them, builds on them and works toward the more complex capabilities sought.

Bruner, on the other hand, *begins* with problem solving, which in turn leads to the development of necessary skills. He poses a problem to be solved (either real or fictitious, specified by the teacher or children, but important to the learners), and uses it as the catalyst to motivate learners to develop the necessary prerequisite skills.

Traditional program sequences and concepts included in the elementary school curriculum generally are derived from the theory espoused by Robert Gagné. Simple mathematical ideas lead to more complex notions and concepts in a spiraling curriculum which begins with kindergarten and continues throughout formal schooling. When writing textbooks, authors analyze prerequisite knowledges and build these into the program before more complex skills are introduced. Curriculum Guides and Scope and Sequence Charts are formulated in much the same way. Programmed texts follow these same procedures but are much more explicit, include a greater number of finitely defined prerequisites, make fewer assumptions about exterior learning experiences (more self-contained), and require much greater control in presentation. Almost all of the mathematical learning we have encountered has been structured in this mode. Teachers have used textbooks as the major mode of instruction and usually the only one other than themselves and a chalkboard. A new concept was introduced related to previous concepts, then students practiced the new idea using problems in the textbook. Periodically, a test was used to assess students' understanding of a series of related concepts.

During the 1960s and 1970s interest accelerated in discovery learning and programs which facilitate such experiences. In England, with support from the Nuffield Foundation and several far-sighted government supervisors, primary schools began experimenting with activity-oriented programs. No specific sequence was specified for pupils to complete. Identifying problems and refining pupil's methods for solving those problems was of paramount importance. *Experiencing* mathematics was the vital ingredient for successful learning.

In the United States the movement was catalyzed through the work of Robert Davis. Davis' position is somewhat between Bruner and Gagné, pressing for discovery but within some structure. He emphasizes the need for directed rather than undirected or open discovery. While not eliminating sequence entirely from the curriculum, he presses for a program in which the student discovers for himself various principles rather than being told those principles.

The third position grows out of Bruner and Piaget, and is not unlike that of the program just described. Recognizing the developmental stages of pupils and their need for concrete materials to help them in developing concepts, these programs are designed around instructional aids. Cuisenaire rods or abaci are two aids which are employed as primary instructional tools and around which programs are designed. Tangrams, geoboards, multibase and attribute blocks are other materials used to develop certain competencies in these programs. Games, puzzles, and specified activities form the basic dimension for materials-oriented instruction.

Mathematics programs, then, are quite varied in scope and reflect a wide variety of learning theories. These are more specifically described in other parts of this volume.

The three psychologists differ somewhat on their concept of readiness. Over a decade has passed since Jerome Bruner wrote ". . . any subject can be taught effectively in some intellectually honest form to any child at any stage of development."[4] Bruner supported this now famous statement by noting that the basic ideas of science and mathematics and the basic themes that give form to life and literature are very simple. Only when these ideas are formalized in terms of equations and complex verbal statements do they become incomprehensible to the young child. Inhelder, who worked closely with Piaget for many years, feels that instruction should accommodate the natural thought processes. Basic ideas of geometry, for example, are appropriate for children in the elementary school provided they are intuitively pursued through material that the child can handle himself rather than through complex mathematical expressions.

Piaget's experiments led him to believe that it was not possible to accelerate the pace of children's readiness very much; the child must be

[4]Jerome S. Bruner, *The Process of Education* (Cambridge, Massachusetts: Harvard University Press, 1962), p. 33.

biologically ready. This view, disputed by many in the United States, would limit education to that appropriate to the child's developmental stage. On the other hand, Bruner's famous pronouncement captures his attitude relative to readiness; he feels that the child is always ready for a concept in some manner. Gagné, on the other hand, relates readiness to the development of sub-skills and sub-concepts rather than to the child's biologic development.

Socio-Cultural Influences

The social and cultural influences on the pupil in the elementary school profoundly affect his attitude, motivation, and development. Teachers often forget the two-thirds of the day when the child is *not* in school. They forget that he spent five formative years before entering the five-seven years in the elementary school. They forget that, for many children, school is an artificial environment which they are compelled to tolerate. Understanding these out-of-school factors which so deeply influence children's lifestyles, actions, and values aids teachers in more effectively teaching them mathematics.

Rapidity of Change

While man has always been in the process of changing, never before has change occurred so rapidly or penetrated every aspect of life so completely. One-fourth of all the people who ever lived are alive today; 90 percent of all scientists and mathematicians who ever lived are alive today. The movement from rural America to megalopolitan regions has accelerated so rapidly that by the year 2000, 75 percent of the population of the United States will be concentrated in urban areas. Less than 10 percent of the population is employed currently in food production while the vast majority was just a hundred years ago. More workers are engaged in the production of services than of goods. The average work day and work week have been shortened, leading to a rapid increase in spectator sports, hobbies, boating, recreation, and vacation homes.

This new and ever-changing world leads to what Alvin Toffler refers to as overchoice. The number and variety of products on the grocer's shelf, entertainment modes, magazines, automobiles—everything we contact—continue to increase. There comes a time when choice, rather than freeing the individual, becomes so complex that it immobilizes him.

We have become the "throw away" generation, Kleenexes, the relative cost of replacing small appliances against repairing them, fads, entertainment and sports heros, clothing styles, and automobiles are designed to be discarded. The feeling of temporariness pervades human relations. One family in four moves each year. People are more concerned with the present than with the future.

Each person has a mental picture of the exterior world, his vision of reality. This not only includes you and us, but the children being taught mathematics. Some of their ideas of reality are fairly correct, others completely wrong. Many will differ from yours. How you deal with them—how and to what extent you develop an understanding of them and use that understanding in the mathematics class—will determine to a great extent your success. *Remember too that today's reality is tomorrow's illusion.* Teachers must work to remain current and relevant.

Family

The structure and influence of the family is changing. Certainly there are more divergent family styles than in any time past. Particularly in urban areas, the traditional family roles are being altered. No longer are children and parents mutually dependent upon one another for emotional support. Children spend a greater portion of time with peers; mothers with neighbors or people who have a common interest; and the whole family watching TV, each person isolated in his own reactions to the screen's events. Physically they are in the same room, emotionally and mentally they are tuned into an electronic device, insulated from each other by a world of noise and action.

Changing roles of men and women also are affecting family life. Women work, sometimes there is no husband in the family, sometimes a succession of "husbands," and sometimes a commune or community of families in the same house. Perhaps, as Alvin Toffler suggests, the population press and increasing governmental control over every aspect of life will become the death knell of the nuclear family unit. For many elementary pupils, this is already a reality. Divorce pervades the suburbs as well as the ghetto. Family pressures on children vary; in the suburbs it is for academic achievement, and the child is motivated by higher grades and other evidences of success; lower-class homes may press the child to neglect school because of its unreality, its lack of any contribution to a vocation, and its drain on the family's earning capacity. The family's influence on the child and the teacher's understanding of that influence, are important in successful teaching.

Consider the mathematics lesson which asks children to compute the distance from Des Moines to San Francisco when the children had never been outside Dallas and had no idea of where Des Moines is or what a distance of a hundred miles means. What about the lesson using airplanes or ships as examples when children had no experience with them. Playing the stock market, dealing with abstract terms, working complex arithmetical problems which have little utility except they fill time—these are but some examples of mathematical lessons which are meaningless to many children, but are taught because they are in a textbook.

Cultural Pluralism

In the past hundred years, America has been characterized as a "melting pot" where masses of immigrants flooding American shores were integrated. This prosaic view was never actually true. As each new wave of immigrants came to this country, they fought for a place. At the turn of the century, for example, signs in Boston proclaimed, "Help Wanted, Irish Need Not Apply." For the blacks who came in slavery, the Chinese brought to build the railroads, and the American Indians beaten in unfair fights and forced onto poor reservations, assimilation was far more difficult and continues today.

In recent years minority peoples have begun to awaken to their own histories and destinies. Their protests against the white power alliance often has led to violence, but in conjunction with court decisions, generated social and political gains. Just as important, it stirred feelings of ethnic price in being black, Chicano, or Native American. This ethnic pride and the cultivation of it is referred to a Cultural Pluralism. America, in this view, is a country where various ethnic, cultural, and religious groups can emphasize and be proud of their unique backgrounds and contributions. No longer would national origins be subjugated in the melting pot theory.

In the cross-cultural currents pervading America, it is likely that you will teach or are teaching in a school where the students come from a subculture other than your own. Rather than blindly imposing your values and ideals, study the community, learn about who the people are, what their life-style is, what they consider important. Instruction derived after such a thoughtful study will profoundly affect the illustrations you use in teaching, the problems posed to develop mathematical competence and the procedures used in instruction.

IIIA.2. Learning Activities

a. Read pages 3–16 in *Teaching Elementary School Mathematics*.
b. Read pages 3–15 in *Teaching Elementary School Mathematics for Understanding*.
c. Read pages 32–58 in *Elementary School Mathematics: A Guide to Current Research*.
d. Read pages 255–60, 263–69, 273–75, 277–82, 293–98 and 309–14 in the April, 1972, issue of *The Arithmetic Teacher*.
e. Conduct one of Piaget's experiments with a child.
f. Find illustrations of at least four of Gagné's eight types of learning and describe them.

IIIA.3. Self-assessment

Turn to objectives IIIA of this Component. If asked to discuss the behavioral science theories specified therein, could you do so? Can you think of ways in which these concepts can be applied to teaching mathematics?

SELECTED BIBLIOGRAPHY FOR ADDITIONAL READING

BRONWELL, ARTHUR B. (ed.). *Science and Technology in the World of the Future.* New York: Wiley-Interscience, 1970.

GAGNÉ, ROBERT M. *The Conditions of Learning.* New York: Holt, Rinehart and Winston, 1964.

HAVIGHURST, ROBERT J. (ed.). *Metropolitanism: Its Challenge to Education,* Sixty-seventh Yearbook, NSSE. Chicago: University of Chicago Press, 1968.

LAMON, WILLIAM E. (ed.). *Learning and the Nature of Mathematics.* Chicago: Science Research Association, 1972.

LOVELL, K. *The Growth of Basic Mathematical and Scientific Concepts in Children.* New York: Philosophical Library, 1961.

PIAGET, JEAN. *The Child's Conception of Number.* New York: Norton, 1941.

PIAGET, JEAN, *et al. The Child's Conception of Geometry.* New York: Basic Books, 1960.

PULASKI, MARY ANN. *Understanding Piaget.* New York: Harper & Row, 1971.

ROSSKOPF, MYRON F., *et al.* (ed.). *Piagetian Cognitive-Development Research and Mathematics Education.* Washington, D.C.: National Council of Teacher of Mathematics, 1971.

TOFFLER, ALVIN. *Future Shock.* New York: Random House, 1970.

Instructional Materials for Elementary School Mathematics Programs

Instructional materials for mathematics programs are those things which the teacher and learner use to facilitate learning. This includes a wide range of materials, from things that are simple and inexpensive (e.g., a bottle top) to things that are complex and expensive (e.g., a computer).

One characteristic of good teaching in mathematics is the effective use of instructional materials. While the research evidence is contradictory and inconclusive, it appears that children learn mathematics more readily when instruction includes manipulation of materials. Teachers who are effective in using such materials feel comfortable with them and continually search for new materials and new ways to use old materials. This component is designed to aid you to make that selection. William Brownell, in a classic experiment which compared use of a variety of instructional devices in England and Scotland, concluded that the teacher's conception of materials was more important than the nature of the materials when pupil achievement was measured.

Component IV has four objectives, the first of which follows.

IVA

> Classify instructional materials according to their concreteness and abstractness.

To get some idea of what this objective is about, do the following:

1. Place five objects (e.g., balls) on a table.
2. Draw a picture of five balls on a piece of paper.
3. Write the numeral 5 on a blank piece of paper.

The five balls are concrete, the drawing is semi-concrete or pictorial, and the numeral is abstract. Research by Piaget, Bruner, and others suggests that the younger the learner, the greater the need for concrete materials. Also, initial concept and/or skill development for most elementary pupils is usually facilitated by beginning the learning sequence with concrete materials.

IVA.1. Instructional Materials

There is no one best classification system for instructional materials used in elementary school mathematics programs. Objects which the learner can manipulate to produce an answer are usually referred to as concrete. However, these may vary in their concreteness. For example, a set of blocks used to show $3 + 2 = \Box$ is more concrete than a number line used for the same purpose. As a rule, the most concrete material is one which the learner manipulates himself and has no built-in abstractions or assumptions. For example, an abacus has the built-in abstraction of place value for the various rows or positions. Therefore, it is not as concrete as a set of sticks that are bundled, even though the learner may manipulate both.

Semi-concrete or pictorial materials are usually materials that the learner observes and does not manipulate. These also vary in their abstractness. For example, the teacher may use a very large abacus to demonstrate or illustrate a mathematical idea. The teacher may manipulate the abacus; but the concreteness of the material is derived from the learner's contact with the material, not the teacher's. An abacus used by the teacher for demonstration purposes, however, is not as abstract as a picture of a set of three birds that cannot be manipulated.

Abstract materials refer to the use of symbols. When teachers use the chalkboard and solve problems using only numerals and signs, abstract materials are being employed. Another illustration of the use of abstract material is the material you have read in this section. It is abstract in that you had to provide meaning for the symbols used in the material. Even here there are degrees of abstractness. Numerals are less abstract than alphabetical symbols used to signify a generalized concept such as $a + b = b + a$. This equation, denoting the commutative property, may represent any pair of numbers in the real number system, and, thus, is somewhat more abstract.

IVA.2. Leaning Activities

a. Read pages 67–76 in *Teaching Elementary School Mathematics*.
b. Read pages 365–82 in *Discovering Meanings in Elementary School Mathematics*.

   c. Read pages 551–58, 592–94 and 596–97 in *The Arithmetic Teacher,* December, 1971.

   d. Review a teacher's edition of a mathematics textbook series. Identify the instructional materials that are recommended.

   e. Visit a teacher's supply store and/or a toy store. Identify the toys/games/materials that might be used to teach mathematical concepts and/or skills.

   f. Look through a catalog, especially one that features teaching materials. Make a list of ten items that could be used to teach mathematics.

   g. Visit an elementary school and discuss instructional materials for mathematics with one of the teachers.

IVA.3. Self-assessment

Make a list of from ten to fifteen instructional materials for mathematics. Rank them according to their concreteness and abstractness. Discuss your list and rankings with a teacher.

IVB

> Illustrate the solution to a given mathematical problem by using a digital instructional material and an analog instructional material.

Digital instructional materials are sometimes referred to as counting materials. Materials of this type form a set whose elements are or can be separated. The process of counting can be used to determine the number of elements in the set.

Analog instructional materials are sometimes referred to as measurement materials. This type of material shows number in a linear form and the process of measuring is used to determine number.

Analog and digital materials can be concrete or pictorial. The concrete/abstract classification system is independent of analog/digital classification. The former refers to the conceptual level and the latter to the form in which number is represented.

IVB.1. Instructional Material

The solution to most arithmetic problems can be illustrated by analog or digital instructional materials. The following are illustrations of the solutions to selected problems:

a. $3 + 2 = \square$

Analog

3	2
5	

$3 + 2 = 5$

Digital

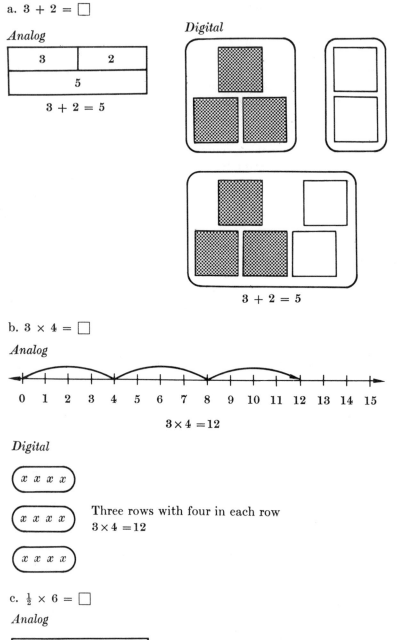

$3 + 2 = 5$

b. $3 \times 4 = \square$

Analog

$3 \times 4 = 12$

Digital

($x\ x\ x\ x$)

($x\ x\ x\ x$)   Three rows with four in each row
$3 \times 4 = 12$

($x\ x\ x\ x$)

c. $\frac{1}{2} \times 6 = \square$

Analog

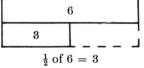

$\frac{1}{2}$ of $6 = 3$

52

Digital

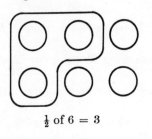

$\frac{1}{2}$ of 6 = 3

d. $\frac{1}{2} \times \frac{3}{4} = \square$

Analog

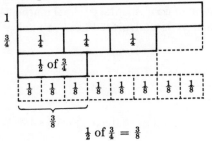

$\frac{1}{2}$ of $\frac{3}{4} = \frac{3}{8}$

Digital

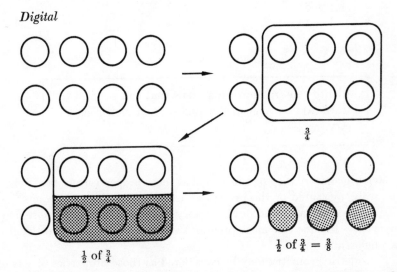

$\frac{1}{2}$ of $\frac{3}{4}$

$\frac{1}{2}$ of $\frac{3}{4} = \frac{3}{8}$

From the preceding exercises, it becomes somewhat apparent that analog materials include the number line and Cuisenaire Rods. Digital materials include blocks, balls, and squares. The learning activities which follow suggest other materials of each type.

IVB.2. Learning Activities

a. Read pages 57–66 and 78–98 in *Teaching Elementary School Mathematics for Understanding.*

b. Read pages 90–132 and 154–81 in *Discovering Meanings in Elementary School Mathematics.*

c. Read page 20 in *Teaching Elementary School Mathematics: What Research Says to the Teacher.*

d. Read pages 149–52 in *The Arithmetic Teacher,* February, 1972.

e. Read pages 259–62 in *The Arithmetic Teacher,* April, 1969.

f. Discuss the use of analog and digital instructional materials with an experienced teacher.

g. Examine the teacher's edition of an elementary school mathematics text series and identify materials and procedures for analog and digital materials.

IVB.3. Self-assessment

Use digital materials and analog materials to illustrate the solutions to the following problems:

a. $5 + \square = 8$ c. $\frac{3}{4} - \frac{1}{2} = \square$

b. $3 \times \square = 15$ d. $\frac{1}{2} \div \frac{1}{4} = \square$

IVC

> Identify instructional materials that can be used to learn (a) metric geometry and (b) non-metric geometry.

Metric geometry may be considered as those properties of sets of points that can be measured or the process of assigning numbers to geometrical entities. It has been a part of the elementary school mathematics program for many years. Included in most programs are the measurement of length, area, angles, and volume.

Non-metric geometry may be considered as those properties of sets of points to which measurement cannot be applied; that is, the concept of measurement is not involved. This aspect of mathematics is relatively new to the elementary school mathematics curriculum. It includes the concepts of point, line segment, line, ray, and curves, open and closed.

IVC.1. Instructional Materials

Metric and measurement geometry require instructional materials that enable the learner to develop an understanding of, and skill in, measuring. The study of linear measures necessitates materials calibrated in inches, feet, and yards. Since the metric system is almost universally used and likely to be adopted soon in the United States, it is essential that linear materials to teach centimeter, decimeter, and meter can be used and understood. Likewise, grams for weight and liters for volume are important concepts to be taught as well as pounds and quarts.

The measurement of area and volume provides many rich opportunities to use instructional materials to discover mathematical formulas. For example, one-inch squares can be used to measure the area of a rectangle. This is not unlike finding the number of pints in a quart and the number of quarts in a gallon.

Non-metric geometry includes the construction of various figures to develop an understanding of the concepts involved. Figures like the following are typically included in the curriculum to be constructed by the learner:

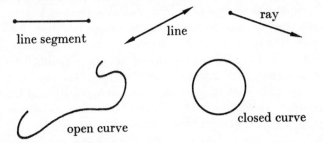

Most figures in a plane can be constructed with a straightedge and/or a compass. Three-dimensional figures present another type of problem. Physical models, some of which can be constructed by folding paper, make a useful instructional material for this area of the curriculum. Suggestions for student activities are included in the readings included below. They provide a rich resource for the elementary teacher of geometry.

IVC.2. Instructional Activities

a. Read pages 318–61 in *Discovering Meanings in Elementary School Mathematics*.
b. Read pages 405–71 in *Teaching Elementary School Mathematics*.
c. Read pages 159–88 in *Teaching Elementary School Mathematics for Understanding*.
d. Read *Readings in Geometry from The Arithmetic Teacher*.

e. Read pages 85–87, 97–104, 117–22 and 127–30 in *The Arithmetic Teacher*, February, 1972.
f. Review a teacher's guide for an elementary school mathematics text series to find what materials are recommended for teaching geometry.

IVC.3. Self-assessment

Select a grade level and make a list of the instructional materials you need to teach metric and non-metric geometry to children at that level. Check your list against the content list found in Component II. Determine if you have materials for teaching all the content areas.

IVD

> List two sets of instructional materials that could be used to teach given mathematical topics.

Teachers select from a wide range of materials those which best meet the needs of the learner. Several different materials are often appropriate in facilitating pupil achievement of an educational objective. Analog materials and digital materials can be used with the same problem, for example. Indeed, sometimes both are used to provide balance and to accommodate varied learning styles. Different kinds of materials should be employed during the different stages of concept development. Materials used to introduce a concept may differ from those needed in application of the concept. And, concept application materials will differ from the concept reinforcement materials that are used in a drill program.

IVD.1. Instructional Materials

Several factors should be considered when making a decision about instructional materials. The factors which you should be prepared to consider at this time are as follows:

a. The age and developmental level of the learner. The material will not be effective if the learner considers the material childish.
b. The stage of development of the concept. Distinctions should be between materials that are best used for (1) concept introduction, (2) concept application, and (3) concept retention or reinforcement.
c. The mathematical topic. Some materials are equally effective with some topics; however, in most cases, one or two materials are most effective for a given topic.
d. The cost of the material. There is no point in spending a large amount of money for materials when a less costly material is equally effective.

It is important for teachers to know and be able to use a variety of instructional materials. Materials will not be equally effective with all learners. Therefore, the teacher needs to be able to identify alternate materials that can be used by the learner.

IVD.2. Instructional Activities

a. Read pages 210–42, 276–84 and 309–403 in *Teaching Elementary School Mathematics.*

b. Read pages 270–301 in *Discovering Meanings in Elementary School Mathematics.*

c. Read pages 99–159 and 189–215 in *Teaching Elementary School Mathematics for Understanding.*

d. Read pages 509–24 in *The Arithmetic Teacher*, October, 1968.

e. Select a concept (e.g., place value, addition of whole numbers). Examine the teacher's edition of a textbook series in elementary school mathematics, a curriculum guide, an elementary school classroom, etc., and make a list of the instructional materials used to teach that concept.

f. Select a popular teaching material (e.g., the abacus, geoboard). Make a list of the concepts that can be taught by the selected teaching material.

g. Interview a classroom teacher. Ask what instructional materials are most effective and for what topic.

IVD.3. Self-assessment

Take the topic: subtraction of whole numbers *or* subtraction of fractional numerals. Considers the topic range to be from the time when it was first introduced to a point where regrouping is required for the solution to a problem. List two complete, but separate (disjoint), sets of instructional materials for the selected topic. Compare your list with that which is found in a methods of teaching elementary school mathematics text.

IVE

> List games and puzzles that can be used to learn mathematics.

Games and puzzles are often considered as enrichment activities. They can be effectively used for that purpose. However, they can also be used as part of the regular program. In most cases, they may be profitably used in the reinforcement or drill aspect of the program.

IVE.1. Instructional Materials

Games and puzzles should be used for an educational purpose. They should facilitate the learner completing a known objective. They are a means to an end, not an end in themselves.

When selecting games and puzzles, it is important to ask the following types of questions:

   a. Can it be used with an individual, a group, or either?
   b. Is it teacher directed or student directed?
   c. What concepts and/or skills are being developed?
   d. What does it cost?
   e. Will it interrupt others?
   f. Is it self-motivating?

IVE.2. Instructional Activities

   a. Examine *Let's Play Games in Mathematics:* Volumes K, 1, 2, 3, 4, 5, 6, and 7 and *Math Games for Greater Achievement.*
   b. Read pages 576–84 in *The Arithmetic Teacher,* December, 1971.
   c. Read pages 211–20 in *Enrichment Mathematics for the Grades.*
   d. Visit a toy store or teacher's supply store and examine the mathematical games.
   e. Read *Arithmetic Games and Activities.*

IVE.3. Self-assessment

Select an age level or a topic in mathematics (e.g., addition) and develop a card file of games and puzzles.

Instructional Diagnosis
of Learning in Mathematics

Instructional diagnosis is the process by which data are collected (by tests, examinations, and observations) and analyzed to formulate instructional objectives for the learner. It enables the teacher to (1) determine the learner's progress in learning, (2) identify his learning difficulties, (3) prescribe objectives for the learner, and (4) design instructional activities.

There is a growing belief that programs in mathematics should be tailored to the learner. Since learning is an individual effort, the programs need to be individualized. To individualize a program in mathematics, the teacher must be able to diagnose the instructional development of the learner. Several competencies make this more feasible. In this Component, you will have an opportunity to develop these competencies.

VA

> Administer and interpret the results of a standardized achievement test in mathematics.

A standardized achievement test, as the name implies, is a nationally normed test that is designed to measure achievement. It is constructed to be given to groups. This does not imply that it could not be given to one person. It could be given to any number of persons at the same time.

Achievement tests in mathematics present sample concepts and/or skills in various areas at several levels of difficulty. The data from the test provide an indication of where the learner is operating within the grade-level sequence. However, since this type of test is designed for groups and is nationally normed, its validity is greater for groups than for a single individual. Therefore, this type of test should only be used in combination with other data when making judgments about individuals; it provides a rough screening which in turn can be refined with other tests.

VA.1. Instructional Materials

Several companies that specialize in test construction publish standardized achievement tests in mathematics. Some of the more popular companies include:

  a. California Test Bureau
  b. Iowa Tests of Educational Development
  c. Metropolitan Achievement Test
  d. Science Research Associates Achievement Series
  e. Stanford Achievement Tests

Most achievement tests in mathematics are separated into sections. For example, the California Arithmetic Test for Grades 4-5-6 has the following sections and subsections:

Arithmetic Reasoning	*Arithmetic Fundamentals*
Meanings	Addition
Signs and Symbols	Subtraction
Problems	Multiplication
	Division

This breakdown of content provides the teacher with some diagnostic data on the learner.

The best way to learn about achievement tests is experience with an achievement test. The following series of learning activities is designed to provide that experience.

VA.2. Instructional Activities

  a. Read pages 27–28 in *Teaching Elementary School Mathematics: What Research Says to the Teacher.*
  b. Read pages 383–98 in *Discovering Meanings in Elementary School Mathematics.*
  c. Examine an achievement test and the teacher's manual for the test.
  d. Select one of the subsections of the test and locate where each item in that subsection is taught in a textbook series.
  e. Role-play giving the test to another adult. Record this activity on audio tape. Play back the audio tape, identifying those areas that may need to be improved.

f. Examine a preadministered achievement test. Rescore the test and recompute the results. Compare your scores with the original scores.

VA.3. Self-assessment

Administer a standardized achievement test in mathematics to a group of at least three learners. Score the tests and analyze the results. Check your results with someone else for accuracy.

VB

> Construct, administer, and analyze the results of a survey test (informal inventory) in mathematics.

A survey test or informal inventory is similar in structure to a standardized achievement test. It differs in that it may not cover as wide a range of topics and *is not* nationally or regionally normed.

The purpose of giving a survey test is to identify areas of difficulty or topics which are causing difficulty. By design, a survey test will not identify a specific learning difficulty. It diagnoses areas of learning, not specific items within the areas.

VB.1. Instructional Materials

Several publishers have developed survey tests which parallel their textbooks. The following is a partial list:

a. Addison-Wesley Publishing Company
b. Holt, Rinehart and Winston, Inc.
c. Science Research Associates, Inc.
d. Scott-Foresman and Company
e. Silver Burdett Company

The following is a sample of a survey test which is concerned with operations with whole numbers.

Addition

1.	25	2.	136	3.	364	4.	726
	$+34$		$+542$		$+357$		357
							804
							$+569$

Subtraction

1.	47	2.	53	3.	642	4.	705
	− 23		− 16		− 265		− 268

Multiplication

1.	23	3.	312	5.	13	7.	47
	× 3		× 4		× 32		× 36

2.	37	4.	605	6.	28	8.	396
	× 2		× 5		× 30		× 608

Division

1. $2\overline{)46}$ 3. $3\overline{)72}$ 5. $6\overline{)407}$ 7. $12\overline{)288}$

2. $3\overline{)156}$ 4. $5\overline{)160}$ 6. $7\overline{)864}$ 8. $53\overline{)3922}$

An examination of the preceding test will show:

  a. The test covers several (in this case, four) areas or topics.
  b. A sampling of items within a area (e.g., addition) is used.
  c. There is a limited, usually small, number of items in each area.
  d. The test items do not repeat. Each one differs in some way from the other items.

A survey test, sometimes called an informal inventory or a survey test, can help the teacher to decide what diagnostic test(s) should be administered. Usually, if one or more items out of four are incorrect, it indicates that a diagnostic test should be given.

VB.2. Instructional Materials

  a. Examine the test in Component I. It has the characteristics of a survey test.
  b. Read pages 385–418 in *Teaching Elementary School Mathematics for Understanding*.
  c. Read pages 67–86 in *A Guide to the Diagnostic Teaching of Arithmetic*.
  d. Examine a commercially prepared survey test.
  e. Most textbook series will contain tests that have the characteristics of a survey test. Locate one of these tests in a textbook series and review its contents.

VB.3. Self-assessment

Select one of the following areas: fractional numerals, metric geometry, or non-metric geometry. Construct a survey test for the selected area.

Administer the test to a group of approximately five learners. Analyze the results. Discuss the process and results with another adult.

VC

> Develop, administer, and analyze the results of a diagnostic test in mathematics.

A diagnostic test is a test designed to identify specific learning difficulties. Whereas a survey test may locate an area of difficulty (e.g., addition of whole numbers), a diagnostic test locates specifically what is known and not known about the addition of whole numbers.

The diagnostic test enables the teacher to focus on specific needs of the learner. This is critical to the individualization of instruction.

VC.1. Instructional Materials

Several textbook and/or test companies distribute commercial diagnostic tests. Representative of these companies are:

a. Bobbs-Merrill Company, Inc.
b. California Test Bureau
c. Educational Testing Service
d. Science Research Associates
e. Scott-Foresman and Company

Certain assumptions are made when preparing a diagnostic test, some of which are:

a. Computation in arithmetic is comprised of a set of specific skills.
b. The skills needed for computation can be ordered according to their difficulty or complexity.
c. The absence of a skill will result in failure of computation requiring that skill.

The following is a sample of part of a diagnostic test in addition of whole numbers:

ADDITION FACTS

Sums <10 *Sums* >9 *and* <15

3	5	6	6	4	5
+2	+4	+1	+7	+8	+9

Sums >14 and <18

8	7	9
+8	+9	+6

Zero addends

0	9	1
+5	+0	+0

Horizontal Form

3 + 2 = ☐   6 + 7 = ☐   5 + 0 = ☐

ADDITION BEYOND THE FACTS

13	12	15	Two-digit plus one digit:
+ 5	+ 6	+ 4	no regrouping

21	33	52	Two-digit plus two-digit:
+32	+41	+37	no regrouping

15	17	18	Two-digit plus one-digit:
+ 7	+ 6	+ 5	with regrouping

(Note: The last two problem sets represent a decision based on which direction the instructional programs take.)

The preceding part of a diagnostic test will provide some ideas concerning the construction of a test of this type. A diagnostic test presents a range of difficulty within a specified area. To be of value, the learner must be able to complete some of the problem sets correctly and must not be able to complete others. The learner should fall somewhere within the range of difficulty presented in the test. This enables the teacher to make judgments about what is known and not known.

An examination of the previous test will show:

a. Three test items are used for each problem type.
b. There is no mixture of problem types within a section of the test.

When analyzing the test, if more than one item in a set of three is missed, this is a good indication that additional work needs to be done in this area.

The discussion of tests, including diagnostic, to this point has focused on testing the learner's understanding of the abstract. Once the abstract level of understanding is determined, an assessment of the concrete should be made. This is done by examining the area where two or three problems were missed. The primary question to be asked is, "Can the learner solve this type of problem if he has a concrete instructional material?" If the answer is "yes," he is ready for one type of instructional program. However, if the answer is "no," he needs a different type of instructional program.

VC.2. Instructional Activities

a. Read pages 42–50 in *Teaching Elementary School Mathematics.*

b. Read pages 399–416 in *Discovering Meanings in Elementary School Mathematics*.

c. Read pages 31–62 and 121–37 in *A Guide to the Diagnostic Teaching of Arithmetic*.

d. Read pages 442–46 in *The Arithmetic Teacher*, May, 1968.

e. Read pages 467–69 in *The Arithmetic Teacher*, November, 1971.

f. Examine a commercially prepared diagnostic test.

g. Review Component II to determine content sequence.

h. Review Component IV to determine materials for the developmental levels.

VC.3. Self-assessment

Select one of the following areas: addition of whole numbers, subtraction of whole numbers, multiplication of whole numbers, division of whole numbers, addition of fractional numerals, subtraction of fractional numerals, multiplication of fractional numerals, and division of fractional numerals. Construct a diagnostic test for the selected area. Administer the test to approximately three learners. Analyze the results of the test. Develop a followup test using manipulative materials. Analyze the results. Discuss the process and results with another adult.

VD

> Develop, administer, and analyze a procedure that would reflect learner attitude toward mathematics.

As children progress through the elementary school, their rating of mathematics becomes lower; kindergarteners rank it first (in most studies) while sixth graders are far less enthusiastic and generally groan when "math time" is announced. Why and how these attitudes are formed is not known. However, one thing is certain: attitudes, positive or negative, affect the learning of mathematics.

VD.1. Instructional Materials

Determining attitudes is difficult and there is no one best approach to the task. Some approaches and sample items include:

a. Multiple choice questionnaire
E.g. I find the subject of mathematics
(1) Exciting
(2) Interesting

    (3) Uninteresting
    (4) Dull
  b. Completion test
    E.g. I find mathematics _____ because
_____.
  c. Comparison with other subjects
    E.g. List the following subjects in the order in which they are most liked to the least liked: spelling, reading, science, mathematics, music.
  d. Adjective checklist
    E.g. Circle each of the words that tell how you most feel about mathematics.

        dull   easy   square
        fun   boring   tough
        hard   cool   worthless
  e. Semantic differential
    E.g. Place a check that best tells your feeling
       distasteful __: __: __: __: __: __ enjoyable
       valuable   __: __: __: __: __: __ worthless
  f. Write a paragraph about how you feel about mathematics.
  g. Interviews
  h. Observations

VD.2. Instructional Activities

  a. Read pages 107–19 in *A Guide to the Diagnostic Teaching of Arithmetic.*
  b. Read pages 631–40 in *The Arithmetic Teacher*, December, 1969.
  c. Read pages 215–20 in *The Arithmetic Teacher*, March, 1969.
  d. Read *Developing Attitude Toward Learning.*
  e. Interview a classroom teacher concerning attitudes toward learning, including mathematics.

VD.3. Self-assessment

Develop a procedure or process for determining attitudes toward mathematics. Use it with a group of three to five students. Analyze the results and draw a conclusion about the students' attitudes. Check your conclusions with a student or someone who knows his academic interest. Then analyze the apparent effectiveness of your instrument in attitude assessment.

VE

> Assimilate, analyze, and interpret diversified data about the learner of mathematics.

No one source of data can provide the teacher with a complete picture of the learner. Teachers use a wide variety of data about their students to provide the best possible learning activities. Therefore, teachers should be able to take a wide array of information and organize it in such a way that a decision about the learner can be made.

VE.1. Instructional Materials

Objectives A, B, C, and D in this Component have considered achievement tests, survey tests, diagnostic tests, and attitude tests. In addition to these tests, most teachers will have available a cumulative record on the learner. The records will usually contain: intelligence (I.Q.) test scores, previous grades, previous test scores, an attendance record, a health record, and some data about the family (e.g., employment, number of children in the family, etc.). These data used in isolation are not so valuable or powerful as when they are used in concert. This usually requires a chart on the learner which reflects all the important data concerning his academic progress in mathematics.

VE.2. Learning Activities

a. Read pages 15–30, 63–65 and 87–106 in *A Guide to the Diagnostic Teaching of Arithmetic.*
b. Examine a student's cumulative record.
c. Talk with a teacher about the sources of data for making educational decisions about learners.

VE.3. Self-assessment

Select one student and collect data that could affect his performance in mathematics directly and indirectly. Include tests that you have prepared and the data from the cumulative record. Analyze the data and write your interpretation of its meaning. Discuss this with an experienced teacher.

Instructional Programs in Mathematics

Three basic approaches have been employed to formulate an instructional program in mathematics. None of the approaches is pure because each uses elements of the others. The three approaches are textbook, individualization, and laboratory. They are called programs because each represents a conceptualized total approach to instruction.

Teachers need to understand and be able to use all three approaches. At this time, a teacher may be employed in a school system or a school using any one of the three. Since it is possible to use elements from each of the programs, teachers should be able to extract those elements which can most profitably be used by the learner.

VIA

> Teach a unit of lessons in mathematics using an elementary school textbook as the primary source.

Most elementary schools use a textbook series in their mathematics program. A textbook series will usually include: a student textbook, a student workbook, supplementary materials, and a teacher's guide. The teacher's guide often reveals the philosophy and psychology of the program. Most teacher's guides suggest instructional materials and activities as well as prescribe the content scope and sequence.

VIA.1. Instructional Materials

Although there are some variations among the various textbook series, most teacher's guides contain these features:

a. Student, program, and/or teacher objectives. These may be given for a unit, a lesson, or both.

b. A list of recommended instructional materials. This will usually include a listing of manipulative aids and teacher demonstration aids.

c. Suggested pre-book activities. These are the introductory (exploratory-motivating-concept development) activities that lead to the activities contained in the student's book. (Some teachers do not use these activities and thereby deprive the learner of some of the more important learning activities. It is most important that the pre-book activities be used if the learner is to have an enjoyable and effective mathematics program.)

d. Textbook activities. These activities are included in the student's book. By the very nature of this medium, the activities are at the pictorial or abstract level.

e. Followup activities. This type of activity is usually (1) additional drill or reinforcement activities that are recommended in order to provide a varied program, e.g., audio-taped drill exercises on the number facts; (2) application activities where the concepts and/or skills are being applied to a "real" world setting, e.g., a field trip to a grocery store; and (3) enrichment activities. These may include puzzles and games designed to extend the depth of understanding of the concept.

f. Evaluation activities. This includes suggested examinations and procedures to evaluate the learner's rate of progress in the program.

g. Answers to the problems presented in the student's book.

The textbook approach is designed primarily for group instruction, not individualized instruction. It assumes that teachers will be teaching groups and, therefore, has the strengths and weaknesses inherent in that type of program design.

VIA.2. Instructional Activities

a. Read pages 31–54 and 419–24 in *Teaching Elementary School Mathematics for Understanding.*

b. Read pages 59–70 in *Elementary School Mathematics: A Guide to Current Research.*

c. Examine a teacher's guide for an elementary school mathematics textbook series.

d. Examine a student's workbook that accompanies an elementary school mathematics series.

e. Discuss, using a teacher's guide, with an experienced teacher.

VIA.3. Self-assessment

Prepare lesson plans for teaching a unit in a mathematics textbook series. Discuss the plans with an experienced teacher and implement them.

VIB

> Operationalize a mathematics laboratory for a small group (6 ± 2) of learners.

A mathematics laboratory is a combination of a setting and an approach. As a setting, it is a location set aside for mathematical experiments and practical activities. As an approach, it is a procedure whereby learners study in an informal manner, select materials, and discover mathematics.

The laboratory approach focuses on the learning activities. It is designed to provide a rich environment for learning and activities that are motivating and stimulating.

VIB.1. Instructional Materials

Mathematics laboratories can be large or small. They can be part of a regular classroom, a designated area in an open space, or a room. The physical facility needs to be as flexible as possible in order that furniture and equipment can be rearranged from time to time. When equipped with a wide range of instructional materials, it can be used by individuals and small groups. No single way to arrange a mathematics laboratory has been found, nor is there any standard list of equipment and supplies. These are dependent on the type of learners who use the laboratory and the purposes of the laboratory.

A mathematics laboratory, as an educational approach, can employ a free discovery methodology or a directed discovery methodology. A free discovery approach allows the learner to explore and experiment without receiving any direction in objectives or materials. A directed discovery approach structures the learner's activities either by prescribing the objectives, materials, activities, or some combination of the three. In application, most mathematics laboratories are a combination of the two approaches.

VIB.2. Instructional Activities

a. Read *The Laboratory Approach to Mathematics.*
b. Read pages 547–50, 559–67 and 585–89 in *The Arithmetic Teacher,* December, 1971.

c. Read pages 7–14 in *The Arithmetic Teacher*, January, 1970.

d. Read pages 105–10 in *The Arithmetic Teacher*, February, 1970.

e. Read pages 372–86 in *The Arithmetic Teacher*, May, 1970.

f. Read pages 501–03 in *The Arithmetic Teacher*, October, 1968.

g. Visit a mathematics laboratory.

h. Review Component IV on instructional materials.

VIB.3. Self-assessment

a. Preoperational Phase
Select an area where a mathematics laboratory might be located. Identify the student who would use the mathematics laboratory. Prepare a scale drawing of the area in the way it could be used as a laboratory, including the furniture and equipment that can be placed in the area. Prepare a materials list.

b. Operational Phase
Operationalize the mathematics laboratory.

VIC

> Prepare and implement a single concept and/or skill program of individualized instruction for three ± one learners.

A program of individualized instruction is a program designed to meet the needs and learning style of an individual learner. The program objectives and activities are formulated on an individual basis. Group activities may be utilized; however, they are used to facilitate meeting an individual objective.

VIC.1. Instructional Materials

This book is an example of an individualized approach to learning. Some of the observable elements that are important are:

a. *Assessment*, including self-assessment, is used to facilitate and direct the learning experiences.

b. *Program objectives* are specific and known to the learner.

c. *Activities* are provided to facilitate the learner's accomplishing the objective. Usually a choice of activities provides the learner with a mode of instruction which corresponds with his learning style.

d. *Evaluation* activities are designed to assess the learner's achievement of the objective.

Several delivery systems are possible for this approach. They include:

a. Computer assisted instruction
b. Programmed textbooks
c. Audio tape material
d. Slide-tape material

VIC.2. Instructional Activities

a. Examine pages 130–82 in *Teaching Elementary School Mathematics*.
b. Read pages 17–27 in *Teaching Elementary School Mathematics*.
c. Read pages 333–56 in *Teaching Elementary School Mathematics for Understanding*.
d. Read pages 5–6, 7–12, 13–16, 17–22, 23–25, and 53–57 in *The Arithmetic Teacher*, January, 1972.
e. Read pages 568–75 in *The Arithmetic Teacher*, December, 1971.
f. Read pages 161–63 in *The Arithmetic Teacher*, March, 1971.
g. Visit a school using Computer Assisted Instruction (CAI).
h. Visit a school using Individually Prescribed Instruction (IPI).

VIC.3. Self-assessment

a. Prepare a written outline of an individualized instruction program.
b. Develop and implement the program.

Instructional Designs
for Teaching Mathematics

An instructional design is a prescription for teaching and learning. The design may include: an ordering of the content, structuring the activities in relation to the concept and/or skill, and an identification of the teacher's role. Two basic design strategies are useful in structuring the sequence of activities in a mathematics lesson—inductive and deductive.

With each of these two strategies, the teacher may be directly involved in instruction or he may employ media to extend his instructional capacity. When the teacher outlines a new concept using the chalkboard, or when he tutors a child, he is directly involved. When a child is sitting in a carrel listening to a recording of number facts and responding to them, the teacher is using a mediated approach.

The instructional design may be viewed as the prescription following the diagnosis. A clinical model of diagnose-prescribe-evaluate is an effective process of instruction. Teachers should be able to employ this model, using the appropriate strategy and teacher role for any given learner.

Regardless of the program approach, the teacher's role, and the strategy employed, it is essential that the design consider the learner's ability and style. Slow learners may not need the same instructions as fast learners and vice versa. Therefore, when designing any instructional activity, it is important to know the learners for which it is intended.

VIIA

> Teach a mathematical concept and/or skill to a small group (4 ± 1) of learners by using a deductive strategy that is teacher-mediated.

A deductive strategy is a design in which the concept and/or skill is communicated very early in the sequence of events in the lesson and then activities are provided to prove, explain, and/or develop the concept. It is a process of starting with an assumption and then dissecting it or analyzing its component parts to develop an understanding of its meaning.

Teacher-mediated is a process in which the teacher has designed the activities and prepared the materials, but is not in direct contact with the learner during the instructional activities. This book is an example of teacher mediation.

VIIA.1. Instructional Materials

A deductive strategy requires progressing from the general and/or abstract to the specific and/or concrete. It is possible, in fact desirable, to use discovery as part of this process. The discovery method of teaching is often thought of in conjunction with the inductive strategy.

To illustrate the deductive strategy, follow a lesson designed to teach the concept of the area of a rectangle. The formula, A (area) = L (length) × W (width), is presented to the learner. Each term is explained, the formula presented, and the process for obtaining necessary data is described. Pupils then may measure objects and compute their areas, but in each instance they employ the formula. Measurement activities are provided in order that the formula can be proved.

VIIA.2. Instructional Activities

a. Read pages 1–15 in *A Guide to Diagnostic Teaching of Arithmetic.*
b. Read pages 28–41 and 51–66 in *Teaching Elementary School Mathematics.*
c. Read pages 417–44 in *Discovering Meanings in Elementary School Mathematics.*
d. Read pages 71–102 in *Elementary School Mathematics: A Guide to Current Research.*
e. Discuss mediated instruction and deductive teaching with an experienced teacher.

VIIA.3. Self-assessment

a. Design the lesson.
b. Develop and produce the lesson.
c. Implement the lesson.
d. Evaluate the lesson. "Did most of the learners complete the objectives for the lesson?"

VIIB

> Teach a mathematical concept and/or skill to a small group (4 ± 1) of learners by using an inductive strategy that is teacher-directed.

An inductive strategy is a design in which the concept and/or skill is learned from the activities that are provided. It is a process of starting with an activity that potentially will enable the learner to discover the objectives and concepts of the lesson. In learning the formula, $L \times W = A$, children using the inductive approach might be given foot-square blocks and asked to determine the area of a table, a room, a wall, or a volleyball court. Questions might be posed such as, "How many feet long and wide is the area?" "Do you find any relation between these measurements and the area of the rectangle?" When the teacher exercises some control of the process, the process is referred to as teacher-directed. This certainly is the case when he provides the foot-square blocks to measure with, the problem to be solved and asks questions which lead learners to the correct solution of the problem.

VIIB.1. Instructional Materials

An inductive process requires moving from the specific or concrete to the general or the abstract. This process is sometimes called discovery; however, it should be understood that discovery could also be used if the process were reversed.

Suppose the concept under consideration is the commutative property of multiplication. By using manipulative materials, learners could determine the products, e.g.,

$3 \times 4 = \square$ is 3 rows of 4

$\qquad$ (x) (x) (x) (x)
$\qquad$ (x) (x) (x) (x)
$\qquad$ (x) (x) (x) (x)

$4 \times 3 = \square$ is 4 rows of 3

$\qquad$ $x \ x \ x$
$\qquad$ $x \ x \ x$
$\qquad$ $x \ x \ x$
$\qquad$ $x \ x \ x$

In each case the product is 12. By repeating this procedure and changing the position of the factors, the learner is able to discover that the order in which the factors appear does not affect the product, or $\triangle \times \square = \square \times \triangle$.

VIIB.2. Instructional Activities

    a. Read pages 278–95 in *The Arithmetic Teacher*, May, 1971.

    b. Read pages 220–24 in *The Arithmetic Teacher*, March, 1970.

    c. Read pages 73–76 in *The Arithmetic Teacher*, February, 1971.

    d. Read pages 503–10 in *The Arithmetic Teacher*, October, 1970.

    e. Observe an experienced teacher while he teaches mathematics. Analyze the teaching strategy.

VIIB.3. Self-assessment

    a. Design the lesson.

    b. Teach the lesson.

    c. Audio tape the lesson as it is being taught.

    d. Analyze and evaluate the audio tape.

    e. Note the strengths and weaknesses in your teaching style.

    f. Evaluate the outcomes of the lesson. "Did most of the learners complete the objectives for the lesson?"

List of References

Books

Brydegaard, Marguerite, and James E. Inskeep, Jr., editors. *Readings in Geometry from The Arithmetic Teacher.* Washington, D.C.: National Council of Teachers of Mathematics, 1970.

*Glennon, Vincent J., and Leroy G. Callahan. *Elementary School Mathematics*, third edition. Washington, D.C.: Association for Supervision and Curriculum Development, NEA, 1968.

*Grossnickle, Foster E., Leo J. Brueckner, and John Reckzen. *Discovering Meanings in Elementary School Mathematics*, fifth edition. New York: Holt, Rinehart and Winston, Inc., 1968.

Hashisaki, Joseph, and John A. Peterson. *Theory of Arithmetic*, third edition. New York: John Wiley and Sons, Inc., 1971.

Henderson, George L. *Math Games for Greater Achievement, Grades 4–9.* Skokie, Illinois: National Textbook Company, 1972.

Henderson, George L., and Adeline Walter. *Let's Play Games in Mathematics, Volumes K-7.* Skokie, Illinois: National Textbook Company, 1970.

Kidd, Kenneth P., Shirley S. Myers, and David M. Ailley. *The Laboratory Approach to Mathematics.* Chicago: Science Research Associates, Inc., 1970.

Lane, Bennie R. *Programmed Guide* to John M. Peterson's *Basic Concepts of Elementary Mathematics.* Boston: Prindle, Weber and Schmidt, Inc., 1971.

*Marks, John L., C. Richard Purdy, and Lucien B. Kinney. *Teaching Elementary School Mathematics for Understanding.* New York: McGraw-Hill Book Company, 1970.

Matchett, Margaret S., and Daniel W. Snader. *Modern Elementary Mathematics.* Boston: Prindle, Weber and Schmidt, Inc., 1971.

Matchett, Margaret S., and Daniel W. Snader. *Tests to Accompany Modern Elementary Mathematics.* Boston: Prindle, Weber and Schmidt, Inc., 1972.

National Council of Teachers of Mathematics. *Enrichment Mathematics for the Grades*, 27th Yearbook. Washington, D.C.: National Council of Teachers of Mathematics, 1963.

Peterson, John M. *Basic Concepts of Elementary Mathematics.* Boston: Prindle, Weber and Schmidt, Inc., 1971.

*Reisman, Fredericka K. *A Guide to the Diagnostic Teaching of Arithmetic.* Columbus, Ohio: Charles E. Merrill Publishing Company, 1972.

Spitzer, Herbert F. *Teaching Elementary School Mathematics.* Washington, D.C.: Association of Classroom Teachers, NEA, 1970.

*Underhill, Robert G. *Teaching Elementary School Mathematics.* Columbus, Ohio: Charles E. Merrill Publishing Co., 1972.

Wagner, Guy, Max Hosier, and Laura Gilloly. *Arithmetic Games and Activities.* Darien, Connecticut: Teacher Publishing Corporation, 1970.

(Note: *These books are used repeatedly throughout the book.)

Periodicals

Component III

Dequette, Raymond J. "Some Thoughts on Piaget's Findings and the Teaching of Fractions," *The Arithmetic Teacher.* Volume 19, Number 4 (April, 1972), pp. 273–75.

Inskeep, James E. "Building a Case for the Application of Piaget's Theory and Research in the Classroom," *The Arithmetic Teacher.* Volume 19, Number 4 (April, 1972), pp. 255–60

Lovell, Kenneth R. "Intellectual Growth and Understanding Mathematics: Implications for Teaching," *The Arithmetic Teacher.* Volume 19, Number 4 (April, 1972), pp. 277–82.

Rosskopf, Myron F. "Using Research in Teaching" in *Piaget Research and the School Mathematics Program,* edited by C. Alan Riedesel, *The Arithmetic Teacher.* Volume 19, Number 4 (April, 1972), pp. 309–14.

Sawada, Daiyo. "Piaget and Pedagogy: Fundamental Relationships," *The Arithmetic Teacher.* Volume 19, Number 4 (April, 1972), pp. 293–98.

Weaver, J. Fred. "Some Concerns about the Application of Piaget's Theory and Research to Mathematical Learning and Instruction," *The Arithmetic Teacher.* Volume 19, Number 4 (April, 1972), pp. 263–69.

Component IV

Armstrong, Jenny R., and Harold Schmidt. "Simple Materials for Teaching Early Number Concepts to Trainable-level Mentally Retarded Pupils," *The Arithmetic Teacher.* Volume 19, Number 2 (February, 1972), pp. 149–52.

Bruni, James V. "A 'Limited' Approach to the Sum of the Angles of a Triangle," *The Arithmetic Teacher.* Volume 19, Number 2 (February, 1972), pp. 85–87.

Coltharp, Forrest L. "Properties of Polygonal Regions," *The Arithmetic Teacher.* Volume 19, Number 2 (February, 1972), pp. 117–22.

D'Augustine, Charles H. "Multiple Methods of Teaching Operations," *The Arithmetic Teacher.* Volume 16, Number 4 (April, 1969), pp. 259–62.

Davidson, Patricia S. "An Annotated Bibliography of Suggested Manipulative Devices," *The Arithmetic Teacher,* Volume 15, Number 6 (October, 1968), pp. 509–24.

Immerzeel, George, and Don Wiederanders. "Ideas," *The Arithmetic Teacher.* Volume 18, Number 8 (December, 1971), pp. 576–84.

LEESEBERG, NORBERT H. "Evaluation Scale for a Teaching Aid in Modern Mathematics," *The Arithmetic Teacher*. Volume 18, Number 8 (December, 1971), pp. 592–94.

LULLI, HENRY. "Polyhedra Construction," *The Arithmetic Teacher*. Volume 19, Number 2 (February, 1972), pp. 127–30.

REYS, ROBERT E. "Considerations for Teachers Using Manipulative Materials," *The Arithmetic Teacher*. Volume 18, Number 8 (December, 1971), pp. 551–58.

SILVERMAN, HELENE. "Where Are the Children?" *The Arithmetic Teacher*. Volume 18, Number 8 (December, 1971), pp. 596–97.

WILLIFORD, HAROLD. "What Does Research Say about Geometry in the Elementary School" in *Rising Research in Teaching*, edited by C. ALAN RIEDESEL, *The Arithmetic Teacher*. Volume 19, Number 2 (February, 1972), pp. 97–104.

COMPONENT V

CAPPS, LELON R., and LINDA SIMON COX. "Attitude Toward Arithmetic at the Fourth- and Fifth-Grade Levels" in *Focus on Research*, edited by C. ALAN RIEDESEL and LEN PAKAART, *The Arithmetic Teacher*. Volume 16, Number 3 (March, 1969), pp. 215–20.

NEALE, DANIEL C. "The Role of Attitudes in Learning Mathematics" in *Focus on Research*, edited by C. ALAN RIEDESEL and LEN PAKAART, *The Arithmetic Teacher*. Volume 16, Number 8 (December, 1969), pp. 631–40.

ROBERTS, GERHARD H. "The Failure Strategies of Third-Grade Arithmetic Pupils" in *Focus on Research*, edited by C. ALAN RIEDESEL and LEN PAKAART, *The Arithmetic Teacher*. Volume 15, Number 5 (May, 1968), pp. 442–46.

WEST, TOMMIE A. "Diagnosing Pupil Errors: Looking for Patterns," *The Arithmetic Teacher*. Volume 18, Number 7 (November, 1971), pp. 467–69.

COMPONENT VI

DAVIDSON, PATRICIA S., and ARLENE W. FAIR. "A Mathematics Laboratory—From Dream to Reality," *The Arithmetic Teacher*. Volume 17, Number 2 (February, 1970), pp. 105–10.

THE EDITORIAL PANEL. "One Point of View: Individualized Instruction," *The Arithmetic Teacher*. Volume 19, Number 1 (January, 1972), pp. 5–6.

EWBANK, WILLIAM A. "The Mathematics Laboratory: What? Why? When? How?" *The Arithmetic Teacher*. Volume 18, Number 8 (December, 1971), pp. 559–67.

GALTON, GRACE K. "Individualized Instruction: Speaking from Reality," *The Arithmetic Teacher*. Volume 19, Number 1 (January, 1972), pp. 23–25.

GRAHAM, EVELYNE M. "Individualized Instruction: Distinguishing Characteristics," *The Arithmetic Teacher*. Volume 19, Number 1 (January, 1972), pp. 13–16.

HENDERSON, GEORGE L. "Individualized Instruction: Sweet in Theory, Sour in Practice," *The Arithmetic Teacher*. Volume 19, Number 1 (January, 1972), pp. 17–22.

LEEB-LUNDBERG, KRISTINA. "Kindergarten Mathematics Laboratory—Nineteenth-Century Fashion," *The Arithmetic Teacher*. Volume 17, Number 5 (May, 1970), pp. 372–86.

MATTHEWS, GEOFFREY, and JULIA COMBER. "Mathematics Laboratories," *The Arithmetic Teacher*. Volume 18, Number 8 (December, 1971), pp. 547–50.

MAY, LOLA J. "Learning Laboratories in Elementary Schools in Winnetka," *The Arithmetic Teacher*. Volume 15, Number 6 (October, 1968), pp. 501–03.

OGILVIE, LLOYD J. "An Individualized Mathematics Program in Junior High School," *The Arithmetic Teacher*. Volume 19, Number 1 (January, 1972), pp. 53–57.

———. "Projects on Individualizing Instruction," *The Arithmetic Teacher*. Volume 18, Number 3 (March, 1971), pp. 161–63.

SCHAEFER, ANNE W., and ALBERT H. MAUTHE. "Problem Solving with Enthusiasm—The Mathematics Laboratory," *The Arithmetic Teacher*. Volume 17, Number 9 (January, 1970), pp. 7–14.

TRAFTON, PAUL R. "Individualized Instruction: Developing Broadened Perspectives," *The Arithmetic Teacher*. Volume 19, Number 1 (January, 1972), pp. 7–12.

VANCE, JAMES H., and THOMAS E. KIEREN. "Laboratory Settings in Mathematics: What does Research Say to the Teacher?" in *Using Research in Teaching*, edited by C. ALAN RIEDESEL, *The Arithmetic Teacher*. Volume 18, Number 8 (December, 1971), pp. 585–89.

WALBESSER, HENRY H. "An Annotated Bibliography of Programmed Instruction in Elementary Mathematics," *The Arithmetic Teacher*. Volume 18, Number 8 (December, 1971), pp. 568–75.

COMPONENT VII

BIGGS, EDITH E., and MAURINE L. HARTUNG. "What's *Your* Position on . . . the Role of Experience in the Learning of Mathematics?" *The Arithmetic Teacher*. Volume 18, Number 5 (May, 1971), pp. 278–95.

JONES, PHILLIP S. "GJY Insert: Discovery Teaching—From Socrates to Modernity," *The Arithmetic Teacher*. Volume 17, Number 6 (October, 1970), pp. 503–10.

KESSLER, BERNARD M. "A Discovery Approach to the Introduction of Flowcharting in the Elementary Grades," *The Arithmetic Teacher*. Volume 17, Number 3 (March, 1970), pp. 220–24.

SMITH, LEWIS B. "A Discovery Lesson in Elementary Mathematics," *The Arithmetic Teacher*. Volume 18, Number 2 (February, 1917), pp. 73–76.